Houston Astros 2021

A Baseball Companion

Edited by Steven Goldman and Bret Sayre

Baseball Prospectus

Craig Brown, Associate Editor
Robert Au, Harry Pavlidis and Amy Pircher, Statistics Editors

Copyright © 2021 by DIY Baseball, LLC.
All rights reserved

This book or any part thereof may not be reproduced or transmitted in any form or by any means, electronic or mechanical, including photocopying, recording, or by any information storage and retrieval system, without permission in writing from the publisher.

Limit of Liability/Disclaimer of Warranty: While the publisher and the author have used their best efforts in preparing this book, they make no representations or warranties with respect to the accuracy or completeness of the contents of this book and specifically disclaim any implied warranties of merchantability or fitness for a particular purpose. No warranty may be created or extended by sales representatives or written sales materials. The advice and strategies contained herein may not be suitable for your situation. You should consult with a professional where appropriate. Neither the publisher nor the author shall be liable for any loss of profit or any other commercial damages, including but not limited to special, incidental, consequential, or other damages.

Library of Congress Cataloging-in-Publication Data:
paperback
ISBN-13: 978-1-950716-45-6

Project Credits
Cover Design: Ginny Searle
Interior Design and Production: Amy Pircher, Robert Au
Layout: Amy Pircher, Robert Au

Baseball icon courtesy of Uberux, from https://www.shareicon.net/author/uberux

Ballpark diagram courtesy of Lou Spirito/THIRTY81 Project, https://thirty81project.com/

Manufactured in the United States of America
10 9 8 7 6 5 4 3 2 1

Table of Contents

Statistical Introduction v

Part 1: Team Analysis
Performance Graphs 3
2020 Team Performance 4
2021 Team Projections 5
Team Personnel 6
Minute Maid Park Stats 7
Astros Team Analysis 9

Part 2: Player Analysis
Astros Player Analysis 16
Astros Prospects 87

Part 3: Featured Articles
Astros All-Time Top 10 Players 99
   by Matthew Trueblood

A Taxonomy of 2020 Abnormalities 105
   by Rob Mains

Tranches of WAR 111
   by Russell A. Carleton

Secondhand Sport 117
   by Patrick Dubuque

Steve Dalkowski Dreaming 121
   by Steven Goldman

A Reward For A Functioning Society 125
   by Cory Frontin and Craig Goldstein

Index of Names 129

Statistical Introduction

Sports are, fundamentally, a blend of athletic endeavor and storytelling. Baseball, like any other sport, tells its stories in so many ways: in the arc of a game from the stands or a season from the box scores, in photos, or even in numbers. At Baseball Prospectus, we understand that statistics don't replace observation or any of baseball's stories, but complement everything else that makes the game so much fun.

What stats help us with is with patterns and precision, variance and value. This book can help you learn things you may not see from watching a game or hundred, whether it's the path of a career over time or the breadth of the entire MLB. We'd also never ask you to choose between our numbers and the experience of viewing a game from the cheap seats or the comfort of your home; our publication combines running the numbers with observations and wisdom from some of the brightest minds we can find. But if you *do* want to learn more about the numbers beyond what's on the backs of player jerseys, let us help explain.

Offense

We've revised our methodology for determining batting value. Long-time readers of the book will notice that we've retired True Average in favor of a new metric: Deserved Runs Created Plus (DRC+). Developed by Jonathan Judge and our stats team, this statistic measures everything a player does at the plate–reaching base, hitting for power, making outs, and moving runners over–and puts it on a scale where 100 equals league-average performance. A DRC+ of 150 is terrific, a DRC+ of 100 is average and a DRC+ of 75 means you better be an excellent defender.

DRC+ also does a better job than any of our previous metrics in taking contextual factors into account. The model adjusts for how the park affects performance, but also for things like the talent of the opposing pitcher, value of different types of batted-ball events, league, temperature and other factors. It's able to describe a player's expected offensive contribution than any other statistic we've found over the years, and also does a better job of predicting future performance as well.

The other aspect of run-scoring is baserunning, which we quantify using Baserunning Runs. BRR not only records the value of stolen bases (or getting caught in the act), but also accounts for all the stuff that doesn't show up on the back of a baseball card: a runner's ability to go first to third on a single, or advance on a fly ball.

Defense

Where offensive value is *relatively* easy to identify and understand, defensive value is ... not. Over the past dozen years, the sabermetric community has focused mostly on stats based on zone data: a real-live human person records the type of batted ball and estimated landing location, and models are created that give expected outs. From there, you can compare fielders' actual outs to those expected ones. Simple, right?

Unfortunately, zone data has two major issues. First, zone data is recorded by commercial data providers who keep the raw data private unless you pay for it. (All the statistics we build in this book and on our website use public data as inputs.) That hurts our ability to test assumptions or duplicate results. Second, over the years it has become apparent that there's quite a bit of "noise" in zone-based fielding analysis. Sometimes the conclusions drawn from zone data don't hold up to scrutiny, and sometimes the different data provided by different providers don't look anything alike, giving wildly different results. Sometimes the hard-working professional stringers or scorers might unknowingly inflict unconscious bias into the mix: for example good fielders will often be credited with more expected outs despite the data, and ballparks with high press boxes tend to score more line drives than ones with a lower press box.

Enter our Fielding Runs Above Average (FRAA). For most positions, FRAA is built from play-by-play data, which allows us to avoid the subjectivity found in many other fielding metrics. The idea is this: count how many fielding plays are made by a given player and compare that to expected plays for an average fielder at their position (based on pitcher ground ball tendencies and batter handedness). Then we adjust for park and base-out situations.

When it comes to catchers, our methodology is a little different thanks to the laundry list of responsibilities they're tasked with beyond just, well, catching and throwing the ball. By now you've probably heard about "framing" or the art of making umpires more likely to call balls outside the strike zone for strikes. To put this into one tidy number, we incorporate pitch tracking data (for the years it exists) and adjust for important factors like pitcher, umpire, batter and home-field advantage using a mixed-model approach. This grants us a number for how many strikes the catcher is personally adding to (or subtracting from) his pitchers' performance ... which we then convert to runs added or lost using linear weights.

Framing is one of the biggest parts of determining catcher value, but we also take into account blocking balls from going past, whether a scorer deems it a passed ball or a wild pitch. We use a similar approach—one that really benefits from the pitch tracking data that tells us what ends up in the dirt and what doesn't. We also include a catcher's ability to prevent stolen bases and how well they field balls in play, and *finally* we come up with our FRAA for catchers.

Pitching

Both pitching and fielding make up the half of baseball that isn't run scoring: run prevention. Separating pitching from fielding is a tough task, and most recent pitching analysis has branched off from Voros McCracken's famous (and controversial) statement, "There is little if any difference among major-league pitchers in their ability to prevent hits on balls hit in the field of play." The research of the analytic community has validated this to some extent, and there are a host of "defense-independent" pitching measures that have been developed to try and extract the effect of the defense behind a hurler from the pitcher's work.

Our solution to this quandary is Deserved Run Average (DRA), our core pitching metric. DRA seeks to evaluate a pitcher's performance, much like earned run average (ERA), the tried-and-true pitching stat you've seen on every baseball broadcast or box score from the past century, but it's very different. To start, DRA takes an event-by-event look at what the pitchers does, and adjusts the value of that event based on different environmental factors like park, batter, catcher, umpire, base-out situation, run differential, inning, defense, home field advantage, pitcher role and temperature. That mixed model gives us a pitcher's expected contribution, similar to what we do for our DRC+ model for hitters and FRAA model for catchers. (Oh, and we also consider the pitcher's effect on basestealing and on balls getting past the catcher.)

DRA is set to the scale of runs allowed per nine innings (RA9) instead of ERA, which makes DRA's scale slightly higher than ERA's. Because of this, for ease of use, we're supplying DRA-, which is much easier for the reader to parse. As with DRC+, DRA- is an "index" stat, meaning instead of using some arbitrary and shifting number to denote what's "good," average is always 100. The reason that it uses a minus rather than a plus is because like ERA, a lower number is better. Therefore a 75 DRA- describes a performance 25 percent better than average, whereas a 150 DRA- means that either a pitcher is getting extremely lucky with their results, or getting ready to try a new pitch.

Since the last time you picked up an edition of this book, we've also made a few minor changes to DRA to make it better. Recent research into "tunneling"—the act of throwing consecutive pitches that appear similar from a batter's point of view until after the swing decision point–data has given us a new contextual factor to account for in DRA: plate distance. This refers to the distance between successive pitches as they approach the plate, and while it has a smaller effect than factors like velocity or whiff rate, it still can help explain pitcher strikeout rate in our model.

Recently Added Descriptive Statistics

Returning to our 2021 edition of the book are a few figures which recently appeared. These numbers may be a little bit more familiar to those of you who have spent some time investigating baseball statistics.

Fastball Percentage

Our fastball percentage (FA%) statistic measures how frequently a pitcher throws a pitch classified as a "fastball," measured as a percentage of overall pitches thrown. We qualify three types of fastballs:

1. The traditional four-seam fastball;
2. The two-seam fastball or sinker;
3. "Hard cutters," which are pitches that have the movement profile of a cut fastball and are used as the pitcher's primary offering or in place of a more traditional fastball.

For example, a pitcher with a FA% of 67 throws any combination of these three pitches about two-thirds of the time.

Whiff Rate

Everybody loves a swing and a miss, and whiff rate (Whiff%) measures how frequently pitchers induce a swinging strike. To calculate Whiff%, we add up all the pitches thrown that ended with a swinging strike, then divide that number by a pitcher's total pitches thrown. Most often, high whiff rates correlate with high strikeout rates (and overall effective pitcher performance).

Called Strike Probability

Called Strike Probability (CSP) is a number that represents the likelihood that all of a pitcher's pitches will be called a strike while controlling for location, pitcher and batter handedness, umpire and count. Here's how it works: on each pitch, our model determines how many times (out of 100) that a similar pitch was called for a strike given those factors mentioned above, and when normalized for each batter's strike zone. Then we average the CSP for all pitches thrown by a pitcher in a season, and that gives us the yearly CSP percentage you see in the stats boxes.

As you might imagine, pitchers with a higher CSP are more likely to work in the zone, where pitchers with a lower CSP are likely locating their pitches outside the normal strike zone, for better or for worse.

Projections

Many of you aren't turning to this book just for a look at what a player has done, but for a look at what a player is going to do: the PECOTA projections. PECOTA, initially developed by Nate Silver (who has moved on to greater fame as a political analyst), consists of three parts:

1. Major-league equivalencies, which use minor-league statistics to project how a player will perform in the major leagues;
2. Baseline forecasts, which use weighted averages and regression to the mean to estimate a player's current true talent level; and
3. Aging curves, which uses the career paths of comparable players to estimate how a player's statistics are likely to change over time.

With all those important things covered, let's take a look at what's in the book this year.

Team Prospectus

Most of this book is composed of team chapters, with one for each of the 30 major-league franchises. On the first page of each chapter, you'll see a box that contains some of the key statistics for each team as well as a very inviting stadium diagram.

We start with the team name, their unadjusted 2020 win-loss record, and their divisional ranking. Beneath that are a host of other team statistics. **Pythag** presents an adjusted 2020 winning percentage, calculated by taking runs scored per game (**RS/G**) and runs allowed per game (**RA/G**) for the team, and running them through a version of Bill James' Pythagorean formula that was refined and improved by David Smyth and Brandon Heipp. (The formula is called "Pythagenpat," which is equally fun to type and to say.)

Next up is **DRC+**, described earlier, to indicate the overall hitting ability of the team either above or below league-average. Run prevention on the pitching side is covered by **DRA** (also mentioned earlier) and another metric: Fielding Independent Pitching (**FIP**), which calculates another ERA-like statistic based on strikeouts, walks, and home runs recorded. Defensive Efficiency Rating (**DER**) tells us the percentage of balls in play turned into outs for the team, and is a quick fielding shorthand that rounds out run prevention.

After that, we have several measures related to roster composition, as opposed to on-field performance. **B-Age** and **P-Age** tell us the average age of a team's batters and pitchers, respectively. **Payroll** is the combined team payroll for all on-field players, and Doug Pappas' Marginal Dollars per Marginal Win (**M$/MW**) tells us how much money a team spent to earn production above replacement level.

Next to each of these stats, we've listed each team's MLB rank in that category from first to 30th. In this, first always indicates a positive outcome and 30th a negative outcome, except in the case of salary—first is highest.

After the franchise statistics, we share a few items about the team's home ballpark. There's the aforementioned diagram of the park's dimensions (including distances to the outfield wall), a graphic showing the height of the wall from the left-field pole to the right-field pole, and a table showing three-year park factors for the stadium. The park factors are displayed as indexes where 100 is average, 110 means that the park inflates the statistic in question by 10 percent, and 90 means that the park deflates the statistic in question by 10 percent.

On the second page of each team chapter, you'll find three graphs. The first is **Payroll History** and helps you see how the team's payroll has compared to the MLB and divisional average payrolls over time. Payroll figures are current as of January 1, 2021; with so many free agents still unsigned as of this writing, the final 2021 figure will likely be significantly different for many teams. (In the meantime, you can always find the most current data at Baseball Prospectus' Cot's Baseball Contracts page.)

The second graph is **Future Commitments** and helps you see the team's future outlays, if any.

The third graph is **Farm System Ranking** and displays how the Baseball Prospectus prospect team has ranked the organization's farm system since 2007.

After the graphs, we have a **Personnel** section that lists many of the important decision-makers and upper-level field and operations staff members for the franchise, as well as any former Baseball Prospectus staff members who are currently part of the organization. (In very rare circumstances, someone might be on both lists!)

Position Players

After all that information and a thoughtful bylined essay covering each team, we present our player comments. These are also bylined, but due to frequent franchise shifts during the offseason, our bylines are more a rough guide than a perfect accounting of who wrote what.

Each player is listed with the major-league team that employed him as of early January 2021. If a player changed teams after that point via free agency, trade, or any other method, you'll be able to find them in the chapter for their previous squad.

As an example, take a look at the player comment for Padres shortstop Fernando Tatis Jr.: the stat block that accompanies his written comment is at the top of this page. First we cover biographical information (age is as of June 30, 2021) before moving onto the stats themselves. Our statistic columns include standard identifying information like **YEAR**, **TEAM**, **LVL** (level of affiliated play) and **AGE** before getting into the numbers. Next, we provide raw, untranslated

Fernando Tatis Jr. SS

Born: 01/02/99   Age: 22   Bats: R   Throws: R
Height: 6'3"   Weight: 217   Origin: International Free Agent, 2015

YEAR	TEAM	LVL	AGE	PA	R	2B	3B	HR	RBI	BB	K	SB	CS	AVG/OBP/SLG
2018	SA	AA	19	394	77	22	4	16	43	33	109	16	5	.286/.355/.507
2019	SD	MLB	20	372	61	13	6	22	53	30	110	16	6	.317/.379/.590
2020	SD	MLB	21	257	50	11	2	17	45	27	61	11	3	.277/.366/.571
2021 FS	SD	MLB	22	600	95	24	4	31	81	50	165	17	8	.263/.331/.499
2021 DC	SD	MLB	22	628	100	25	4	32	85	53	173	19	8	.263/.331/.499

Comparables: Darryl Strawberry, Bo Bichette, Ronald Acuña Jr.

YEAR	TEAM	LVL	AGE	PA	DRC+	BABIP	BRR	FRAA	WARP
2018	SA	AA	19	394	136	.370	3.0	SS(83): -1.9	2.4
2019	SD	MLB	20	372	118	.410	7.1	SS(83): 0.9	3.4
2020	SD	MLB	21	257	126	.306	0.7	SS(57): -5.5	0.9
2021 FS	SD	MLB	22	600	126	.318	1.7	SS -1	3.9
2021 DC	SD	MLB	22	628	126	.318	1.8	SS -1	4.0

numbers like you might find on the back of your dad's baseball cards: **PA** (plate appearances), **R** (runs), **2B** (doubles), **3B** (triples), **HR** (home runs), **RBI** (runs batted in), **BB** (walks), **K** (strikeouts), **SB** (stolen bases) and **CS** (caught stealing).

Following the basic stats is **Whiff%** (whiff rate), which denotes how often, when a batter swings, he fails to make contact with the ball. Another way to think of this number is an inverse of a hitter's contact rate.

Next, we have unadjusted "slash" statistics: **AVG** (batting average), **OBP** (on-base percentage) and **SLG** (slugging percentage). Following the slash line is **DRC+** (Deserved Runs Created Plus), which we described earlier as total offensive expected contribution compared to the league average.

BABIP (batting average on balls in play) tells us how often a ball in play fell for a hit, and can help us identify whether a batter may have been lucky or not ... but note that high BABIPs also tend to follow the great hitters of our time, as well as speedy singles hitters who put the ball on the ground.

The next item is **BRR** (Baserunning Runs), which covers all of a player's baserunning accomplishments including (but not limited to) swiped bags and failed attempts. Next is **FRAA** (Fielding Runs Above Average), which also includes the number of games previously played at each position noted in parentheses. Multi-position players have only their two most frequent positions listed here, but their total FRAA number reflects all positions played.

Our last column here is **WARP** (Wins Above Replacement Player). WARP estimates the total value of a player, which means for hitters it takes into account hitting runs above average (calculated using the DRC+ model), BRR and FRAA. Then, it makes an adjustment for positions played and gives the player a credit for plate appearances based upon the difference between "replacement level"—which is derived from the quality of players added to a team's roster after the start of the season–and the league average.

The final line just below the stats box is **PECOTA** data, which is discussed further in a following section.

Catchers

Catchers are a special breed, and thus they have earned their own separate box which displays some of the defensive metrics that we've built just for them. As an example, let's check out Yasmani Grandal.

YEAR	TEAM	P. COUNT	FRM RUNS	BLK RUNS	THRW RUNS	TOT RUNS
2018	LAD	16816	15.7	0.8	0.1	16.5
2019	MIL	18740	19.4	1.8	-0.1	21.1
2020	CHW	4830	3.7	0.3	-0.2	3.8
2021	CHW	14430	16.7	-0.6	1.0	17.1
2021	CHW	14430	16.7	0.4	1.0	18.0

The **YEAR** and **TEAM** columns match what you'd find in the other stat box. **P. COUNT** indicates the number of pitches thrown while the catcher was behind the plate, including swinging strikes, fouls and balls in play. **FRM RUNS** is the total run value the catcher provided (or cost) his team by influencing the umpire to call strikes where other catchers did not. **BLK RUNS** expresses the total run value above or below average for the catcher's ability to prevent wild pitches and passed balls. **THRW RUNS** is calculated using a similar model as the previous two statistics, and it measures a catcher's ability to throw out basestealers but also to dissuade them from testing his arm in the first place. It takes into account factors like the pitcher (including his delivery and pickoff move) and baserunner (who could be as fast as Billy Hamilton or as slow as Yonder Alonso). **TOT RUNS** is the sum of all of the previous three statistics.

Pitchers

Let's give our pitchers a turn, using 2020 AL Cy Young winner Shane Bieber as our example. Take a look at his stat block: the first line and the **YEAR**, **TEAM**, **LVL** and **AGE** columns are the same as in the position player example earlier.

Here too, we have a series of columns that display raw, unadjusted statistics compiled by the pitcher over the course of a season: **W** (wins), **L** (losses), **SV** (saves), **G** (games pitched), **GS** (games started), **IP** (innings pitched), **H** (hits allowed) and **HR** (home runs allowed). Next we have two statistics that are rates: **BB/9** (walks per nine innings) and **K/9** (strikeouts per nine innings), before returning to the unadjusted K (strikeouts).

Next up is **GB%** (ground ball percentage), which is the percentage of all batted balls that were hit on the ground, including both outs and hits. Remember, this is based on observational data and subject to human error, so please approach this with a healthy dose of skepticism.

BABIP (batting average on balls in play) is calculated using the same methodology as it is for position players, but it often tells us more about a pitcher than it does a hitter. With pitchers, a high BABIP is often due to poor defense or bad luck, and can often be an indicator of potential rebound, and a low BABIP may be cause to expect performance regression. (A typical league-average BABIP is close to .290-.300.)

The metrics **WHIP** (walks plus hits per inning pitched) and **ERA** (earned run average) are old standbys: WHIP measures walks and hits allowed on a per-inning basis, while ERA measures earned runs on a nine-inning basis. Neither of these stats are translated or adjusted.

DRA- (Deserved Run Average) was described at length earlier, and measures how the pitcher "deserved" to perform compared to other pitchers. Please note that since we lack all the data points that would make for a "real" DRA for minor-league events, the DRA- displayed for minor league partial-seasons is based off of different data. (That data is a modified version of our cFIP metric, which you can find more information about on our website.)

Shane Bieber   RHP

Born: 05/31/95   Age: 26   Bats: R   Throws: R
Height: 6'3"   Weight: 200   Origin: Round 4, 2016 Draft (#122 overall)

YEAR	TEAM	LVL	AGE	W	L	SV	G	GS	IP	H	HR	BB/9	K/9	K	GB%	BABIP
2018	AKR	AA	23	3	0	0	5	5	31	26	1	0.3	8.7	30	47.3%	.278
2018	COL	AAA	23	3	1	0	8	8	48^2	30	3	1.1	8.7	47	52.0%	.227
2018	CLE	MLB	23	11	5	0	20	19	114^2	130	13	1.8	9.3	118	46.2%	.356
2019	CLE	MLB	24	15	8	0	34	33	214^1	186	31	1.7	10.9	259	44.4%	.298
2020	CLE	MLB	25	8	1	0	12	12	77^1	46	7	2.4	14.2	122	48.4%	.267
2021 FS	CLE	MLB	26	10	6	0	26	26	150	121	18	2.1	11.7	195	45.5%	.297
2021 DC	CLE	MLB	26	14	7	0	30	30	196.7	159	24	2.1	11.7	257	45.5%	.297

Comparables: Luis Severino, Danny Salazar, Joe Musgrove

YEAR	TEAM	LVL	AGE	WHIP	ERA	DRA-	WARP	MPH	FB%	WHF	CSP
2018	AKR	AA	23	0.87	1.16	61	0.9				
2018	COL	AAA	23	0.74	1.66	69	1.2				
2018	CLE	MLB	23	1.33	4.55	74	2.6	94.7	57.4%	26.2%	
2019	CLE	MLB	24	1.05	3.28	75	4.9	94.4	45.8%	30.8%	
2020	CLE	MLB	25	0.87	1.63	53	2.6	95.3	53.6%	40.7%	
2021 FS	CLE	MLB	26	1.04	2.44	64	4.4	94.7	50.0%	33.2%	44.2%
2021 DC	CLE	MLB	26	1.04	2.44	64	5.8	94.7	50.0%	33.2%	44.2%

Just like with hitters, **WARP** (Wins Above Replacement Player) is a total value metric that puts pitchers of all stripes on the same scale as position players. We use DRA as the primary input for our calculation of WARP. You might notice that relief pitchers (due to their limited innings) may have a lower WARP than you were expecting or than you might see in other WARP-like metrics. WARP does not take leverage into account, just the actions a pitcher performs and the expected value of those actions ... which ends up judging high-leverage relief pitchers differently than you might imagine given their prestige and market value.

MPH gives you the pitcher's 95th percentile velocity for the noted season, in order to give you an idea of what the *peak* fastball velocity a pitcher possesses. Since this comes from our pitch-tracking data, it is not publicly available for minor-league pitchers.

Finally, we display the three new pitching metrics we described earlier. **FB%** (fastball percentage) gives you the percentage of fastballs thrown out of all pitches. **WHF** (whiff rate) tells you the percentage of swinging strikes induced out of all pitches. **CSP** (called strike probability) expresses the likelihood of all pitches thrown to result in a called strike, after controlling for factors like handedness, umpire, pitch type, count and location.

PECOTA

All players have PECOTA projections for 2021, as well as a set of other numbers that describe the performance of comparable players according to PECOTA. All projections for 2021 are for the player at the date we went to press in early January and are projected into the league and park context as indicated by the team abbreviation. (Note that players at very low levels of the minors are too unpredictable to assess using these numbers.) All PECOTA projected statistics represent a player's projected major-league performance.

How we're doing that is a little different this season. There are really two different values that go into the final stat line that you see for PECOTA: How a player performs, and how much playing time he'll be given to perform it. In the past we've estimated playing time based on each team's roster and depth charts, and we'll continue to do that. These projections are denoted as **2021 DC**.

But in many cases, a player won't be projected for major-league playing time; most of the time this is because they aren't projected to be major-league players at all, but still developing as prospects. Or perhaps a player will provide Triple-A depth, only to have an opportunity open up because of injury. For these purposes, we're also supplying a second projection, labeled **2021 FS**, or full season. This is what we would project the player to provide in 600 plate appearances or 150 innings pitched.

Below the projections are the player's three highest-scoring comparable players as determined by PECOTA. All comparables represent a snapshot of how the listed player was performing at the same age as the current player, so if a

23-year-old pitcher is compared to Bartolo Colón, he's actually being compared to a 23-year-old Colón, not the version that pitched for the Rangers in 2018, nor to Colón's career as a whole.

A few points about pitcher projections. First, we aren't yet projecting peak velocity, so that column will be blank in the PECOTA lines. Second, projecting DRA is trickier than evaluating past performance, because it is unclear how deserving each pitcher will be of his anticipated outcomes. However, we know that another DRA-related statistic–contextual FIP or cFIP–estimates future run scoring very well. So for PECOTA, the projected DRA- figures you see are based on the past cFIPs generated by the pitcher and comparable players over time, along with the other factors described above.

If you're familiar with PECOTA, then you'll have noticed that the projection system often appears bullish on players coming off a bad year and bearish on players coming off a good year. (This is because the system weights several previous seasons, not just the most recent one.) In addition, we publish the 50th percentile projections for each player–which is smack in the middle of the range of projected production—which tends to mean PECOTA stat lines don't often have extreme results like 40 home runs or 250 strikeouts in a given season. In essence, PECOTA doesn't project very many extreme seasons.

Managers

After all those wonderful team chapters, we've got statistics for each big-league manager, all of whom are organized by alphabetical order. Here you'll find a block including an extraordinary amount of information collected from each manager's entire career. For more information on the acronyms and what they mean, please visit the Glossary at www.baseballprospectus.com.

There is one important metric that we'd like to call attention to, and you'll find it next to each manager's name: **wRM+** (weighted reliever management plus). Developed by Rob Arthur and Rian Watt, wRM+ investigates how good a manager is at using their best relievers during the moments of highest leverage, using both our proprietary DRA metric as well as Leverage Index. wRM+ is scaled to a league average of 100, and a wRM+ of 105 indicates that relievers were used approximately five percent "better" than average. On the other hand, a wRM+ of 95 would tell us the team used its relievers five percent "worse" than the average team.

While wRM+ does not have an extremely strong correlation with a manager, it is statistically significant; this means that a manager is not *entirely* responsible for a team's wRM+, but does have some effect on that number.

Part 1: Team Analysis

Performance Graphs

Payroll History (in millions)

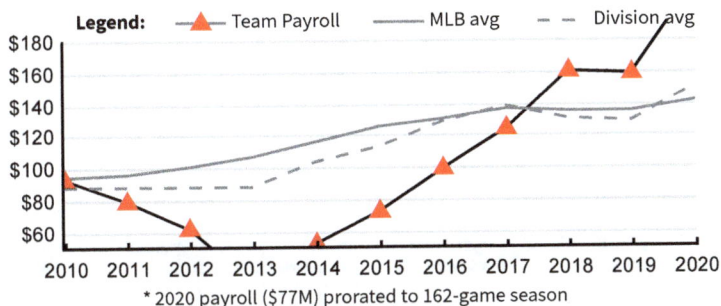

*2020 payroll ($77M) prorated to 162-game season

Future Commitments (in millions)

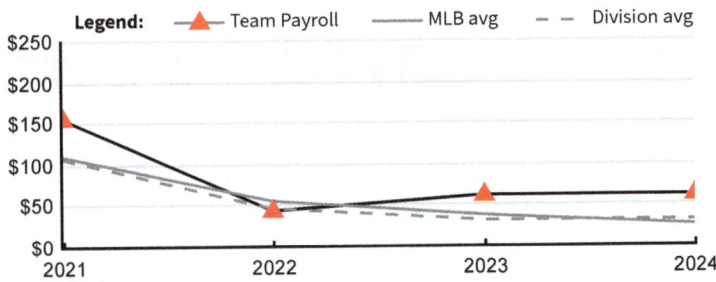

Farm System Ranking

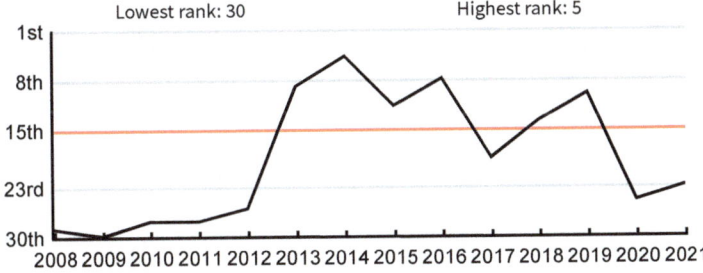

2020 Team Performance

ACTUAL STANDINGS

Team	W	L	Pct
OAK	36	24	0.600
HOU	**29**	**31**	**0.483**
SEA	27	33	0.450
LAA	26	34	0.433
TEX	22	38	0.367

dWIN% STANDINGS

Team	W	L	Pct
OAK	29	31	0.499
LAA	29	31	0.497
HOU	**28**	**32**	**0.472**
SEA	22	38	0.370
TEX	18	42	0.304

TOP HITTERS

Player	WARP
Kyle Tucker	1.4
George Springer	1.3
Michael Brantley	0.9

TOP PITCHERS

Player	WARP
Framber Valdez	1.8
Zack Greinke	1.3
Lance McCullers Jr.	1.1

VITAL STATISTICS

Statistic Name	Value	Rank
Pythagenpat	.507	12th
dWin%	.472	14th
Runs Scored per Game	4.65	14th
Runs Allowed per Game	4.58	14th
Deserved Runs Created Plus	102	13th
Deserved Run Average Minus	97	13th
Fielding Independent Pitching	4.36	11th
Defensive Efficiency Rating	.707	7th
Batter Age	29.7	25th
Pitcher Age	27.4	7th
Payroll	$77.0M	4th
Marginal $ per Marginal Win	$5.4M	22nd

2021 Team Projections

PROJECTED STANDINGS

Team	W	L	Pct	+/-
HOU	92.5	69.5	0.571	14
There's reason to be skeptical of the starting pitching depth, but this team will score plenty of runs.				
LAA	86.2	75.8	0.532	16
Still buying pitching from the bargain bin despite a new GM, they lack the depth to be great, but if the stars stay healthy, they'll be good.				
OAK	82.2	79.8	0.507	-15
Free-agent departures in the outfield, infield, and bullpen leave them scrambling for coverage despite Matts Chapman and Olson.				
SEA	70.7	91.3	0.436	-2
The rebuild should be nearly over, but will go on for at least another year after a shockingly silent winter.				
TEX	66.8	95.2	0.412	7
A team in total, chaotic transition, but the kids could be fun to watch.				

TOP PROJECTED HITTERS

Player	WARP
Alex Bregman	4.9
Jose Altuve	3.8
Yordan Alvarez	3.4

TOP PROJECTED PITCHERS

Player	WARP
Zack Greinke	3.8
Framber Valdez	2.5
Lance McCullers Jr.	2.3

FARM SYSTEM REPORT

Top Prospect	Number of Top 101 Prospects
Forrest Whitley, #69	2

KEY DEDUCTIONS

Player	WARP
George Springer	5.3
Rogelio Armenteros	0.3

KEY ADDITIONS

Player	WARP
Pedro Báez	0.7
Joe Smith	0.7
Jason Castro	0.6
Ryne Stanek	0.4

Team Personnel

General Manager
James Click

Assistant GM, Player Development
Pete Putila

Senior Director, Baseball Operations
Armando Velasco

Senior Director, Baseball Strategy
Bill Firkus

Manager
Dusty Baker

BP Alumni
James Click
Ryan Lind

Minute Maid Park Stats

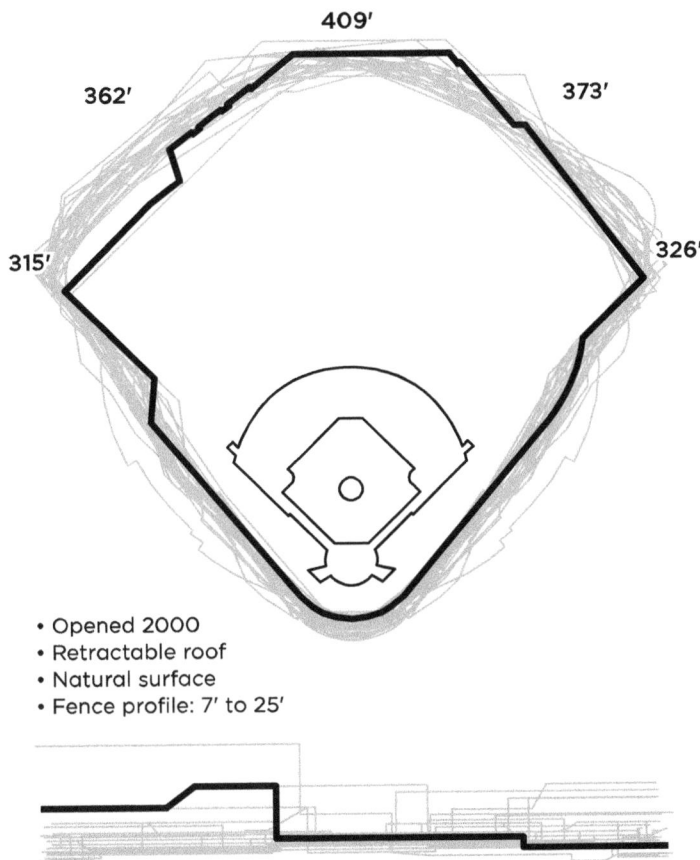

- Opened 2000
- Retractable roof
- Natural surface
- Fence profile: 7' to 25'

Three-Year Park Factors

Runs	Runs/RH	Runs/LH	HR/RH	HR/LH
99	99	99	106	103

Astros Team Analysis

The root of the Houston Astros' success over the last five seasons can be traced to a few of the worst teams ever—or, specifically, to the draft picks they resulted in. Houston built its dynasty through one of the most severe and desolate tank jobs in the sport's history. After three consecutive 100-loss seasons, from 2011-13, the Astros emerged with an overhauled front office, a loaded farm system and the core of a roster that would win 100-plus three years in a row. That bunch would eventually claim a World Series title as well as a pair of pennants.

The goal of then-GM Jeff Luhnow's strategy wasn't to ping-pong between championships and no. 1 picks, of course: it was to build a sustainably competitive franchise, one that could replace core after core and stay strong indefinitely. To make this vision a reality, the Astros constructed one of the greatest player-development machines baseball has seen, amending the league's blueprint along the way, as competitors tried to copy how Houston identified and trained players.

Though Luhnow is now more than a year removed from running the show, following his dismissal stemming from the sign-stealing scandal, the stage is nearly set to test his process—to see if the Astros can transcend the success cycle, even as their core graduates into free agency and/or enters the decline phase of their careers.

The thinking behind the success cycle concept goes like this: success is a blessing, but it's also a curse from a front-office perspective. With each year that a team sits at the top of the league, it subtracts from its draft haul, a drain that is felt most acutely at the top of the first round. Without a supply of top-tier picks, the Astros—and other teams like them—have to do more with less. Whereas, at the beginning of their rebuild, the Astros could passively absorb the best talents in the draft, since becoming a good team they've had to work harder to uncover gems.

This negative feedback loop tends to propel teams toward cycles of contention, establishing windows of three to five years' worth of excellence before a rebuild becomes necessary. And yet, every front office dreams (or ought to dream) of escaping that loop. The notion of a player-development machine so efficient and effective that it can continuously churn out a full roster's worth of high-level major-league talent without requiring sky-high payrolls is the baseball equivalent of a nuclear fusion reactor: It's possible, but nobody has ever managed to make it work.

Sure, the Dodgers and Yankees can contend year after year, and do so partially by continuously graduating talented prospects, but they also supplement their rosters with exorbitant spending. Astros owner Jim Crane plainly doesn't want to match that level of financial investment, meaning Houston has to operate more like the Rays and the Cardinals, two teams who, despite apparent player-development chops, have had to take a down year every once in a while to restock their cupboard (for the Rays, 2016; for the Cardinals, 2017-18).

The Astros arguably made more progress toward baseball's fusion reactor than any team in recent memory. Luhnow and his since-departed lieutenant Sig Mejdal revolutionized the science of player development. As chronicled in Ben Lindbergh and Travis Sawchik's book, The MVP Machine, Mejdal and Luhnow brought new data-gathering instruments to the minors, rewired (and sometimes fired) coaching and scouting staffs and helped bridge the divide between the nerds in the front office and the players on the field. Their tactics ranged from the obvious (telling pitchers to throw their best pitches more frequently) to the arcane (installing high-speed cameras in minor-league parks). Most importantly, they worked—and we have the numbers to prove it.

Measuring development is hard, not least because it's not a linear process. Prospects don't just improve in a steplike fashion, becoming better each year until they're ready for the bigs. It's messy and complicated: they take steps forward and back, adjust to a new league and then get injured, take a successful cup of coffee in the major leagues and then can't hack it in Triple-A. So, we can't rely on the normal measures of progress. The average change in hitting or pitching ability from year to year, for example, means almost nothing when systems thrive or wilt on whether two or three prospects make it. It doesn't matter if a team's Double-A prospects consistently get 2 to 3 percent better each year if that makes them only into better Triple-A roster fillers. Good systems produce major leaguers, not just better minor leaguers.

Instead of concerning ourselves with the average change in skill each year, I used the number of players who break out as the most important metric. This criterion better matches the idea that it's not about the typical grind of development so much as the players taking big steps forward; those are the prospects who show up on rankings, who may make it to the majors and who may even become impact players.

I quantified the idea of a "breakout" by using a threshold of 10 percent better performance from year to year. If a player was league-average in Year One but 110 percent of league-average in Year Two, then that qualifies. A surprisingly small number of prospects meet this criteria: only about 10 percent of all the player-seasons (minimum 200 plate appearances) in the last five years qualify as "breakouts" as I've defined the term. This stability is thanks in part to Baseball Prospectus' Deserved Run Average and Deserved Runs Created statistics, which subtract a lot of the noise and variation that come from small-sample size, players switching leagues or home parks and other factors that make it look like a player has become a hitting god when really they just moved to the PCL.

By this metric, lots of teams are good at hitting development or good at pitching development, but few are great at both. The Cardinals, for example, excel at drawing breakouts out of their batters, as attested to by José Martinez, Paul DeJong and others. The Athletics are not normally known for their pitcher talents, but in recent years they have brought up breakout hurlers like Sonny Gray, Sean Manaea and Jharel Cotton. Houston is the rare example of a team who excels at turning out players both on the mound and in the batter's box.

Name	Year	Change in DRA-
Trent Thornton	2016	-29.75
Evan Grills	2016	-28.58
Trent Thornton	2017	-8.86
Brandon Bailey	2018	-7.19
Cy Sneed	2017	-3.03
Trent Thornton	2018	-2.81
Jose Urquidy	2016	-2.07
Keegan Yuhl	2016	-1.88

Houston pitchers with large improvements in DRA- relative to the prior year (>500 batters faced). Players with bolded names have accrued playing time in MLB.

Name	Year	Percent Improvement (DRC+)	PA
Ramón Laureano	2016	58.27%	555
Daz Cameron	2017	56.56%	522
Taylor Jones	2018	54.06%	530
Osvaldo Duarte	2018	46.07%	535
Corey Julks	2018	37.05%	521
Jason Martin	2017	25.18%	518
Ronnie Dawson	2017	12.21%	518
Derek Fisher	2016	11.55%	566
Josh Rojas	2018	10.41%	556
Kyle Tucker	2017	6.56%	619

Houston players with large improvements in DRC+ relative to the prior year (>500 PA). Players with bolded names have accrued playing time in MLB.

Houston Astros 2021

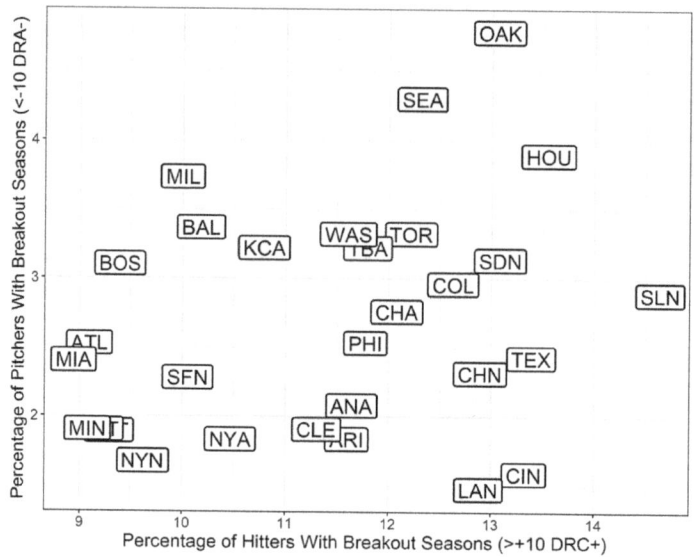

Indeed, no team surpasses their skill in both aspects of development. The Cardinals are in a virtual tie, although due much more to their batsmen than their arms; everyone else is far behind these two teams, which share a common player development DNA by way of Mejdal and Luhnow. Even the vaunted Dodgers, whose core has proven to be every bit as good or better than the Astros since 2015, have leaned less on their homegrown talent. (In some cases, harvesting other teams' talents, like the Dodgers did with Mookie Betts, was the better move than trying to build an outfielder as good in-house.)

All this player-development success has translated into one of the strongest cores of the current era. The Baseball Gauge calculates a "homegrown WAR" metric that measures how many wins above replacement come from players developed by a team. Four of Houston's five squads ranked in the top 20 of all teams since 2015 by this measurement, putting the team far in the lead over the full five-season span. The gap between Houston and second-place Boston in homegrown WAR was roughly the same as the gap between Boston and sixth-place Cleveland, both front offices with their own notable player-development success.

But Houston's recent dominance in this measure doesn't guarantee that they will continue to stay so strong—the coming years appear certain to test their processes in that regard.

The average age of Houston's hitters, according to Baseball Reference, has increased by almost four years since 2015—a byproduct of fielding largely the same group of regulars. The core that powered them to a championship and more than 500 wins in the last six seasons is getting older and starting to show signs of being worse for it, from Josh Reddick's dramatic dropoff (and subsequent departure) to Yuli Gurriel and Jose Altuve's anemic batting in 2020. The Astros are also experiencing the other realities that come with players amassing service time and gaining earning power: Houston lost George Springer to free agency over the winter, and Carlos Correa may follow suit after the 2021 season. The ascents of Kyle Tucker and, before him, Yordan Alvarez should help offset some of those losses, albeit likely not all of them.

The same goes for the pitching side of the equation, where the Astros pieced together a competent-enough and significantly younger rotation after losing Gerrit Cole to the Yankees. A year from now, the Astros may have to replace Justin Verlander, Zack Greinke and Lance McCullers, a significant portion of their innings pitched over the last three years. They survived the loss of Verlander to Tommy John surgery last season, but outside of that and McCullers surgery in 2018, Houston has largely had a run of good injury luck when it comes to starters.

The surprising success of Houston's young pitching shows that they do have a chance to make it work—even without having their top two picks in each of the 2020 and 2021 drafts. The Astros will have to lean on alternate means of talent acquisition. That means producing players like Framber Valdez, the 26-year-old Dominican starter signed as an amateur international free-agent, will take on greater importance. Other promising hurlers have followed similar paths through their system, from Jose Urquidy to Cristian Javier. With any luck, the Astros will hit on another Collin McHugh—a waiver-wire find—or help another Dallas Keuchel—originally a seventh-round pick—reach and prosper at the big-league level with their careful instruction.

As clear as Houston's success in helping improve their hitters and pitchers has been, it's harder to place 2020 in the arc of their story. With little explanation, the Astros went from one of the most dominant teams in history in 2019 to an also-ran that fortuitously made the postseason. But, coming as it did on the heels of morale-crushing revelations about Houston's sign-stealing scheme, perhaps their performance ought to be graded on a curve. After all, Dusty Baker led the team to within a few runs of another World Series appearance. Their playoff run may augur well for their ability to replace lost talent and continue to push deep into future postseasons.

The Astros sure hope so, anyway. Though they've managed to produce some historically great rosters, the coming years will offer their steepest player-development challenge yet. As the current core begins to age out of its productive years, will the Astros be able to replace them? The real crucible for Luhnow's vision was whether they could continuously turn over that level of talent after their tanking ended.

Houston Astros 2021

In 2021, and over the next few seasons, we'll start to see whether Houston is able, under James Click's watch, to realize the modern front office dream of a perpetual contention machine. Or, if like most teams before them, they'll have to start all over again.

—*Rob Arthur is an author of Baseball Prospectus.*

Part 2: Player Analysis

Houston Astros 2021

PLAYER COMMENTS WITH GRAPHS

Jose Altuve   2B
Born: 05/06/90   Age: 31   Bats: R   Throws: R
Height: 5'6"   Weight: 166   Origin: International Free Agent, 2007

YEAR	TEAM	LVL	AGE	PA	R	2B	3B	HR	RBI	BB	K	SB	CS	AVG/OBP/SLG
2018	HOU	MLB	28	599	84	29	2	13	61	55	79	17	4	.316/.386/.451
2019	HOU	MLB	29	548	89	27	3	31	74	41	82	6	5	.298/.353/.550
2020	HOU	MLB	30	210	32	9	0	5	18	17	39	2	3	.219/.286/.344
2021 FS	HOU	MLB	31	600	97	27	2	24	74	49	100	17	6	.289/.359/.480
2021 DC	HOU	MLB	31	641	104	29	2	26	79	53	107	18	7	.289/.359/.480

Comparables: Ian Kinsler, Robinson Canó, Keith Lockhart

    Altuve was one player for whom sign-stealing decline couldn't be offered as a lazy explanation for a poor 2020; the trash can was not banged for him, nor did he see the same improvements in his plate discipline that many colleagues enjoyed. The abbreviated campaign was his worst since his rookie season. While we've seen the power suffer along with his ailing knee before, for the first time ever, he didn't hit for average. That failing can only partly be attributed to BABIP misfortune as Altuve also posted a career-worst strikeout rate. A declining contact trend can be seen all the way back to 2014. The keystone of this team had a lot of leeway beneath him then. Now he's run out of room.

YEAR	TEAM	LVL	AGE	PA	DRC+	BABIP	BRR	FRAA	WARP
2018	HOU	MLB	28	599	126	.352	2.4	2B(130): -7.9	3.2
2019	HOU	MLB	29	548	118	.303	-0.5	2B(121): -0.6, SS(1): -0.0	3.0
2020	HOU	MLB	30	210	78	.250	2.4	2B(48): 2.5	0.4
2021 FS	HOU	MLB	31	600	123	.322	0.8	2B -1, SS 0	3.6
2021 DC	HOU	MLB	31	641	123	.322	0.9	2B -1	3.8

Jose Altuve, continued

Batted Ball Distribution

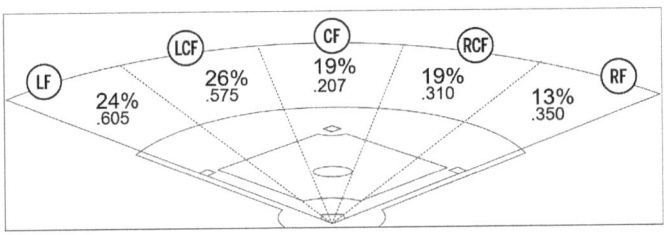

Strike Zone vs LHP   **Strike Zone vs RHP**

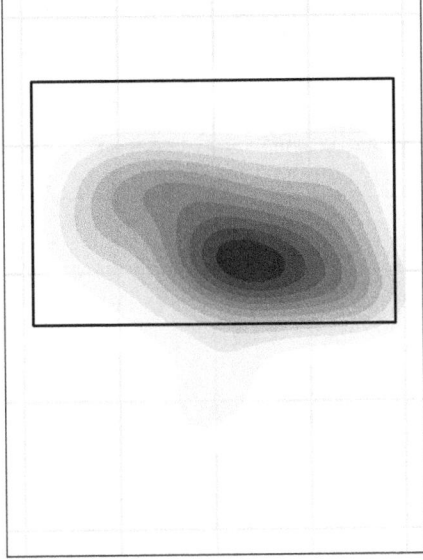

Michael Brantley LF

Born: 05/15/87 Age: 34 Bats: L Throws: L
Height: 6'2" Weight: 209 Origin: Round 7, 2005 Draft (#205 overall)

YEAR	TEAM	LVL	AGE	PA	R	2B	3B	HR	RBI	BB	K	SB	CS	AVG/OBP/SLG
2018	CLE	MLB	31	631	89	36	2	17	76	48	60	12	3	.309/.364/.468
2019	HOU	MLB	32	637	88	40	2	22	90	51	66	3	2	.311/.372/.503
2020	HOU	MLB	33	187	24	15	0	5	22	17	28	2	0	.300/.364/.476
2021 FS	HOU	MLB	34	600	90	32	1	18	79	53	87	8	4	.277/.348/.446
2021 DC	HOU	MLB	34	590	89	31	1	18	77	52	86	8	4	.277/.348/.446

Comparables: Dusty Baker, Shannon Stewart, Kevin McReynolds

Dr. Smooth rolled out his collection of highly successful numbers once again, further distancing himself from a tumultuous mid-career blip with reassuring daily consistency. There are signs of age: for the first time in his career, Brantley occupied a new slot at DH more often than his regular outfield berth, while he came up empty with his hacks a little more often than we're used to. Brantley's still at the top of the game when it comes to playing those hits, which is as good a sign as any that he'll make a slick segue into his role with another station.

YEAR	TEAM	LVL	AGE	PA	DRC+	BABIP	BRR	FRAA	WARP
2018	CLE	MLB	31	631	118	.319	1.4	LF(134): -3.4	2.8
2019	HOU	MLB	32	637	121	.320	0.0	LF(120): -7.4, RF(9): -0.8	2.5
2020	HOU	MLB	33	187	117	.336	-1.1	LF(19): 1.9	0.9
2021 FS	HOU	MLB	34	600	113	.304	-0.1	LF -2, RF 0	2.4
2021 DC	HOU	MLB	34	590	113	.304	-0.1	LF -2	2.2

Michael Brantley, continued

Batted Ball Distribution

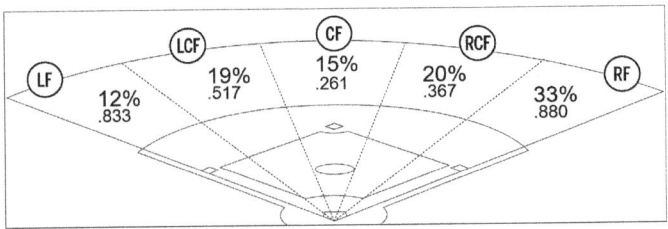

Strike Zone vs LHP   Strike Zone vs RHP

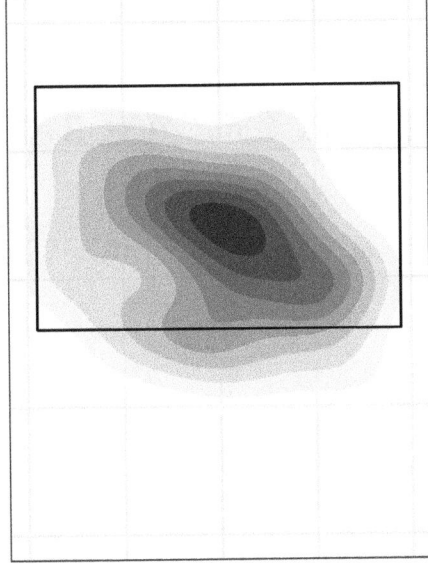

Astros Player Analysis - 19

Houston Astros 2021

Alex Bregman 3B

Born: 03/30/94 Age: 27 Bats: R Throws: R
Height: 6'0" Weight: 192 Origin: Round 1, 2015 Draft (#2 overall)

YEAR	TEAM	LVL	AGE	PA	R	2B	3B	HR	RBI	BB	K	SB	CS	AVG/OBP/SLG
2018	HOU	MLB	24	705	105	51	1	31	103	96	85	10	4	.286/.394/.532
2019	HOU	MLB	25	690	122	37	2	41	112	119	83	5	1	.296/.423/.592
2020	HOU	MLB	26	180	19	12	1	6	22	24	26	0	0	.242/.350/.451
2021 FS	HOU	MLB	27	600	101	31	2	31	95	78	96	7	3	.277/.385/.526
2021 DC	HOU	MLB	27	654	110	33	2	33	103	86	105	8	3	.277/.385/.526

Comparables: Chipper Jones, Eric Chavez, David Wright

The sign-stealing scandal would have been the perfect opportunity for a Bregman heel turn. What we got instead was a series of deflections, followed by a press conference apology as poorly scripted as the clunkiest wrestling promo. The third baseman followed that up with a good, albeit muted season that, like the WWE itself, lacked any intensity without antagonistic fans in attendance. Bregman was something of a tweener to begin with, so perhaps the Astros simply didn't know where to take this storyline. In the absence of a proper apology, let's be honest: it would have been far more entertaining if Bregman had opened that presser by declaring "IT'S ME, MANFRED! IT WAS ME ALL ALONG!"

YEAR	TEAM	LVL	AGE	PA	DRC+	BABIP	BRR	FRAA	WARP
2018	HOU	MLB	24	705	149	.289	-1.6	3B(136): 5.4, SS(28): -0.4, 2B(2): -0.1	7.4
2019	HOU	MLB	25	690	157	.281	-3.8	3B(99): 6.6, SS(65): 4.7	8.6
2020	HOU	MLB	26	180	125	.254	0.3	3B(42): 0.3	0.9
2021 FS	HOU	MLB	27	600	141	.292	-0.1	3B 2, 2B 0	4.6
2021 DC	HOU	MLB	27	654	141	.292	-0.2	3B 2	4.9

Alex Bregman, continued

Batted Ball Distribution

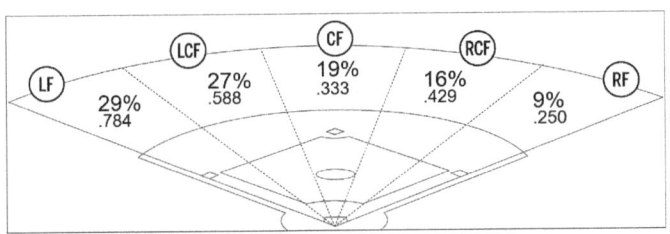

Strike Zone vs LHP   Strike Zone vs RHP

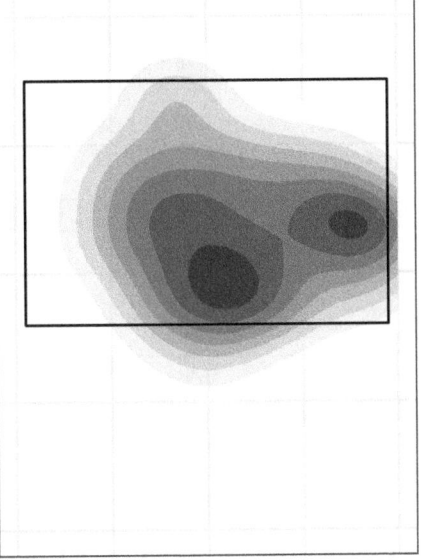

Houston Astros 2021

Jason Castro C
Born: 06/18/87   Age: 34   Bats: L   Throws: R
Height: 6'3"   Weight: 215   Origin: Round 1, 2008 Draft (#10 overall)

YEAR	TEAM	LVL	AGE	PA	R	2B	3B	HR	RBI	BB	K	SB	CS	AVG/OBP/SLG
2018	MIN	MLB	31	74	4	3	0	1	3	9	26	0	0	.143/.257/.238
2019	MIN	MLB	32	275	39	9	0	13	30	33	88	0	0	.232/.332/.435
2020	LAA	MLB	33	62	5	4	0	2	6	10	23	0	0	.192/.323/.385
2020	SD	MLB	33	30	3	5	0	0	3	2	10	0	0	.179/.233/.357
2021 FS	HOU	MLB	34	600	75	24	1	21	70	69	211	1	1	.202/.303/.374
2021 DC	HOU	MLB	34	225	28	9	0	8	26	26	79	0	1	.202/.303/.374

Comparables: Jason LaRue, David Ross, Tom Wilson

Castro was part of the Padres' overhaul of their dismal catching situation at the trade deadline. He departs as he arrived, a serviceable though aging catcher. Unsurprisingly, his defense and framing skills are eroding, and he has struck out in over a third of his plate appearances since 2018. At his age, that isn't going to get any better. On the bright side, plate discipline ages well, and Castro's is still quite good. A team with a need at catcher could do a lot worse than taking a chance on him for 2021.

YEAR	TEAM	P. COUNT	FRM RUNS	BLK RUNS	THRW RUNS	TOT RUNS
2018	MIN	3157	1.4	0.9	0.1	2.3
2019	MIN	10695	6.1	-1.9	-0.3	3.9
2020	SD	1135	0.4	-0.2	0.0	0.1
2020	LAA	2172	0.8	-0.3	0.0	0.5
2021	HOU	8418	3.0	-0.8	0.1	2.3
2021	HOU	8418	3.0	-0.6	0.1	2.5

YEAR	TEAM	LVL	AGE	PA	DRC+	BABIP	BRR	FRAA	WARP
2018	MIN	MLB	31	74	57	.216	-0.7	C(19): 2.5	0.2
2019	MIN	MLB	32	275	100	.307	1.0	C(78): 3.5	1.9
2020	LAA	MLB	33	62	87	.296	-0.3	C(17): -0.3	0.1
2020	SD	MLB	33	30	86	.278	-0.4	C(9): 0.2	0.0
2021 FS	HOU	MLB	34	600	80	.294	-0.7	C 5	1.4
2021 DC	HOU	MLB	34	225	80	.294	-0.3	C 3	0.6

Jason Castro, continued

Batted Ball Distribution

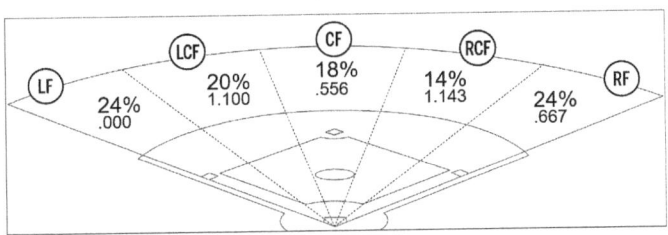

Strike Zone vs LHP   Strike Zone vs RHP

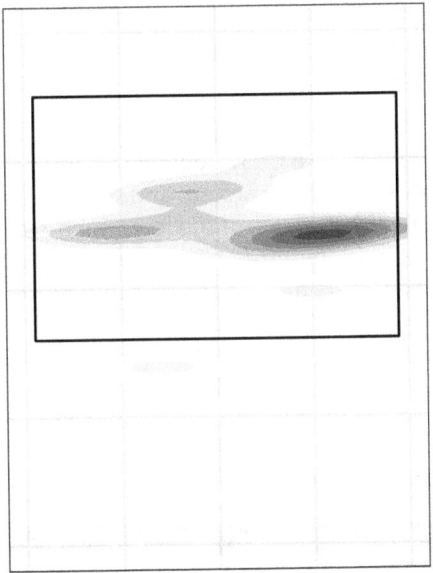

Carlos Correa SS

Born: 09/22/94   Age: 26   Bats: R   Throws: R
Height: 6'4"   Weight: 220   Origin: Round 1, 2012 Draft (#1 overall)

YEAR	TEAM	LVL	AGE	PA	R	2B	3B	HR	RBI	BB	K	SB	CS	AVG/OBP/SLG
2018	HOU	MLB	23	468	60	20	1	15	65	53	111	3	0	.239/.323/.405
2019	HOU	MLB	24	321	42	16	1	21	59	35	75	1	0	.279/.358/.568
2020	HOU	MLB	25	221	22	9	0	5	25	16	49	0	0	.264/.326/.383
2021 FS	HOU	MLB	26	600	83	27	1	26	85	64	137	5	2	.265/.351/.470
2021 DC	HOU	MLB	26	548	76	24	1	24	78	58	125	4	2	.265/.351/.470

Comparables: Corey Seager, Alex Rodriguez, Hanley Ramirez

To paraphrase Correa himself after the Astros dumped the luckless Twins out of the playoffs: what *are* we going to say now? With a standard 10-team postseason format, this comment would have been exploring the disappointment of his offensive performance in a rare season of good health. The expanded bracket instead afforded a sub-.500 team the opportunity to sneak into October and truly infuriate the fans who had already been denied the opportunity to express their disgust at the sign-stealing scheme in person. Correa jumped on that opportunity like a forewarned hitter on a fastball, combining a scorching run at the plate with quotes that cast the Astros as the victims and placed himself firmly at the center of the storm.

It wasn't the first time Correa drew the ongoing vitriol from this saga. He clashed with Cody Bellinger when the Dodgers star suggested Jose Altuve's 2017 MVP award was stolen, and was the target of Joe Kelly's infamous pout that precipitated one of the few bench-clearing incidents of the year. The lightning rod role energized him in a way that it hadn't during the regular season, as his six homers and 1.221 OPS brought Houston to the brink of another World Series. To answer his question: many people are going to say exactly the same thing as they were saying before, responding as vehemently as Correa's personal intensity warrants. No matter what he does, Correa is going to have to deal with the repercussions of the scandal for the rest of his career. If this postseason is the way he responds going forwards, opposing fans are going to have to deal with him being extremely good indeed.

YEAR	TEAM	LVL	AGE	PA	DRC+	BABIP	BRR	FRAA	WARP
2018	HOU	MLB	23	468	98	.282	0.8	SS(109): 7.2	2.8
2019	HOU	MLB	24	321	125	.303	-0.6	SS(75): -2.3	2.3
2020	HOU	MLB	25	221	84	.324	0.1	SS(57): -2.4	-0.1
2021 FS	HOU	MLB	26	600	120	.315	-0.5	SS 0	3.4
2021 DC	HOU	MLB	26	548	120	.315	-0.4	SS 0	3.1

Carlos Correa, continued

Batted Ball Distribution

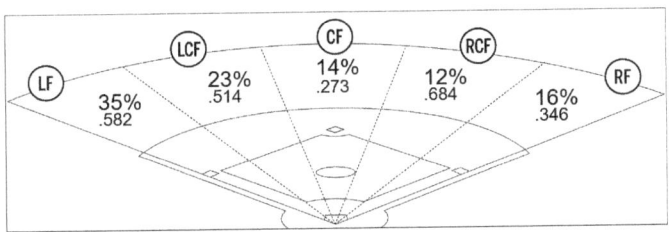

Strike Zone vs LHP   Strike Zone vs RHP

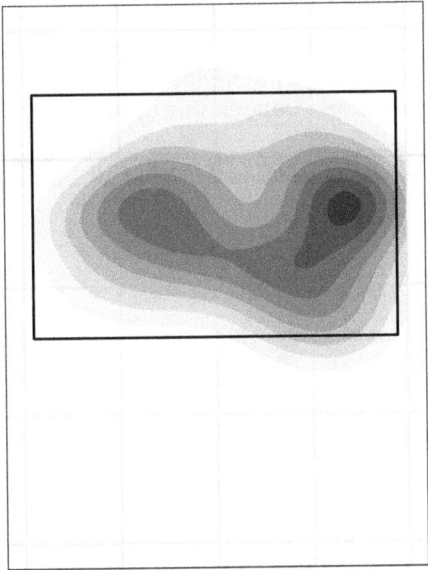

Aledmys Díaz 2B

Born: 08/01/90   Age: 30   Bats: R   Throws: R
Height: 6'1"   Weight: 195   Origin: International Free Agent, 2014

YEAR	TEAM	LVL	AGE	PA	R	2B	3B	HR	RBI	BB	K	SB	CS	AVG/OBP/SLG
2018	TOR	MLB	27	452	55	26	0	18	55	23	62	3	4	.263/.303/.453
2019	HOU	MLB	28	247	36	12	1	9	40	26	28	2	0	.271/.356/.467
2020	HOU	MLB	29	59	8	5	0	3	6	1	12	0	0	.241/.254/.483
2021 FS	HOU	MLB	30	600	78	27	1	23	80	42	106	5	3	.250/.314/.431
2021 DC	HOU	MLB	30	234	30	10	0	9	31	16	41	2	1	.250/.314/.431

Comparables: Miguel Tejada, J.J. Hardy, Alexei Ramirez

Good utility players need to be able to bide their time and be ready whenever called upon. Houston appeared to have coaxed a higher level of plate discipline out of Díaz, a development that promised a productive season ahead. A groin strain sorely tested that patience as the utilityman was forced to miss a month after appearing in just one game. Upon his return, Díaz slipped back into his free-swinging ways, chasing in areas he shouldn't as though he was trying to cram a season's worth of production into a fraction of the time. His approach still resulted in some powerful moments, but success was rare when it came to reaching base. He didn't even swing any more often; he just picked the wrong pitches to go after. Díaz will need to recapture his 2019 composure at the plate if he's to be a dependable utility bat and not an all-or-nothing wildcard.

YEAR	TEAM	LVL	AGE	PA	DRC+	BABIP	BRR	FRAA	WARP
2018	TOR	MLB	27	452	107	.269	-1.8	SS(95): -5.8, 3B(38): -0.5	1.5
2019	HOU	MLB	28	247	108	.268	1.9	1B(26): -0.8, 2B(25): 0.6, 3B(19): -0.8	1.1
2020	HOU	MLB	29	59	98	.256	0.0	2B(10): -0.1, 3B(3): -0.2, 1B(2): 0.2	0.1
2021 FS	HOU	MLB	30	600	97	.275	-0.3	2B 1, SS 0	1.3
2021 DC	HOU	MLB	30	234	97	.275	-0.1	2B 0, SS 0	0.6

Aledmys Díaz, continued

Batted Ball Distribution

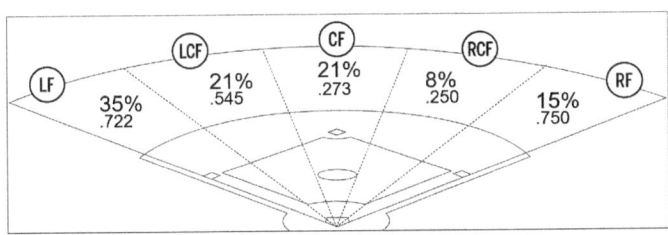

Strike Zone vs LHP   Strike Zone vs RHP

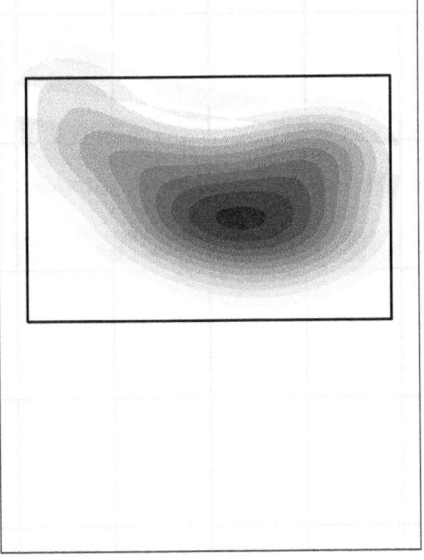

Yuli Gurriel 1B

Born: 06/09/84 Age: 37 Bats: R Throws: R
Height: 6'0" Weight: 215 Origin: International Free Agent, 2016

YEAR	TEAM	LVL	AGE	PA	R	2B	3B	HR	RBI	BB	K	SB	CS	AVG/OBP/SLG
2018	HOU	MLB	34	573	70	33	1	13	85	23	63	5	1	.291/.323/.428
2019	HOU	MLB	35	612	85	40	2	31	104	37	65	5	3	.298/.343/.541
2020	HOU	MLB	36	230	27	12	1	6	22	12	27	0	1	.232/.274/.384
2021 FS	HOU	MLB	37	600	76	32	1	22	89	29	85	4	3	.269/.314/.448
2021 DC	HOU	MLB	37	552	70	29	1	20	82	26	78	4	2	.269/.314/.448

Comparables: Steve Garvey, Eric Karros, Cecil Cooper

In notorious sabermetric masterpiece *Bull Durham*, Crash Davis foresaw our future fixation on BABIP when highlighting the difference between hitting .250 and .300: one hit a week. Crash would have approved of Gurriel's democratic approach to strikeouts but, for all his sage advice, he had little to say on the topic of how to turn a season around when there's a mere 10 weeks to work with. Gurriel squeezed every ounce of juice out of the 2019 ball and then suffered a drastic reversal of fortunes, an object lesson in how a 60-game sample can affect even the most dependable hitter. Almost everything was identical to his career numbers: the strikeout, walk, and swing rates; exit velocity and launch angle; DRC+. Almost. The one thing that didn't hold up was the production itself. Few of Gurriel's flares, gorks, or dying quails seemed to materialize in hits, condemning him to career worsts in all three slash line components. Baseball's shortest season only proved the inescapable truth of Crash's words: one more dying quail per week would have seen Gurriel hit .280.

YEAR	TEAM	LVL	AGE	PA	DRC+	BABIP	BRR	FRAA	WARP
2018	HOU	MLB	34	573	109	.306	1.1	1B(109): 1.5, 3B(21): 1.2, 2B(15): -1.0	2.0
2019	HOU	MLB	35	612	119	.289	-1.5	1B(110): 7.3, 3B(42): 0.4, 2B(4): -0.2	3.4
2020	HOU	MLB	36	230	107	.235	-0.8	1B(55): 4.6	0.8
2021 FS	HOU	MLB	37	600	101	.287	-0.5	1B 3, 2B 0	1.3
2021 DC	HOU	MLB	37	552	101	.287	-0.5	1B 3	1.1

Yuli Gurriel, continued

Batted Ball Distribution

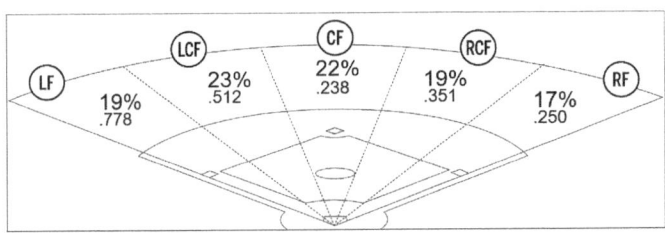

Strike Zone vs LHP   Strike Zone vs RHP

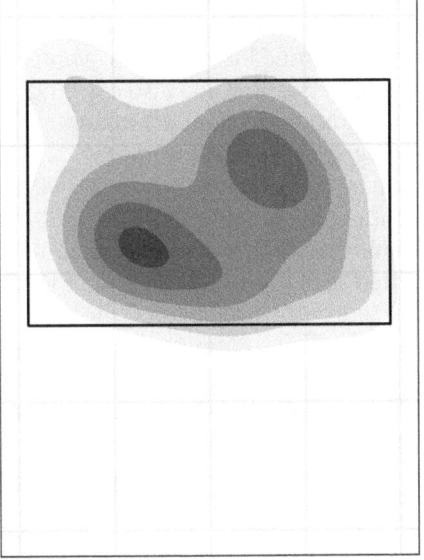

Martín Maldonado C

Born: 08/16/86 Age: 34 Bats: R Throws: R
Height: 6'0" Weight: 230 Origin: Round 27, 2004 Draft (#803 overall)

YEAR	TEAM	LVL	AGE	PA	R	2B	3B	HR	RBI	BB	K	SB	CS	AVG/OBP/SLG
2018	LAA	MLB	31	290	24	14	0	5	32	13	73	0	1	.223/.284/.332
2018	HOU	MLB	31	114	15	4	1	4	12	3	25	0	0	.231/.257/.398
2019	HOU	MLB	32	98	20	4	0	6	10	13	26	0	0	.202/.316/.464
2019	KC	MLB	32	263	26	15	0	6	17	17	55	0	0	.227/.291/.366
2019	CHC	MLB	32	13	0	0	0	0	0	2	5	0	0	.000/.154/.000
2020	HOU	MLB	33	165	19	4	0	6	24	27	51	1	0	.215/.350/.378
2021 FS	HOU	MLB	34	600	75	20	1	20	69	54	178	2	1	.203/.294/.362
2021 DC	HOU	MLB	34	346	43	11	0	12	39	31	102	0	1	.203/.294/.362

Comparables: Ron Karkovice, Todd Pratt, Chris Gimenez

YEAR	TEAM	P. COUNT	FRM RUNS	BLK RUNS	THRW RUNS	TOT RUNS
2018	HOU	4771	1.7	-0.3	0.2	1.6
2018	LAA	11404	4.1	-0.8	0.3	3.7
2019	KC	10492	-1.4	3.3	0.3	2.1
2019	CHC	571	-0.1	-0.3	0.0	-0.3
2019	HOU	3403	-0.5	0.9	-0.3	0.1
2020	HOU	6449	-1.4	0.3	-0.2	-1.4
2021	HOU	13228	1.5	1.8	1.1	4.4
2021	HOU	13228	1.5	1.8	1.1	4.4

Ahead of Game 7 of the ALCS, Lance McCullers praised Maldonado's "will to win" and "grit." That might sound like Hawk Harrelson excusing a poor offensive performance with intangibles, but Maldonado three-true-outcomed his way to an average offensive season while also carrying out an impressive feat of pitcher management that is somewhat unquantifiable. Let's try anyway. Fifteen rookies pitched for the Astros in 2020, a number only matched by the COVID-depleted Marlins. Those rookies ended up pitching more than half of Houston's innings, leading the league. Maldonado guided the newcomers through the vast majority, handling almost three-quarters of the time behind the plate. He then started all but one of the team's playoff games—entering the other for the final four innings—to shepherd this rookie-reliant pitching staff within one game of the World Series. The Astros believed in Maldonado enough to not only bring him back to the team for the third time in three years but also to entrust him with almost all of their catching work. While his statistical résumé as a framer appears to be getting less impressive as he ages, his colleagues will tell you he excels at practically everything else.

YEAR	TEAM	LVL	AGE	PA	DRC+	BABIP	BRR	FRAA	WARP
2018	LAA	MLB	31	290	74	.287	-0.1	C(77): 1.1	0.6
2018	HOU	MLB	31	114	75	.263	-0.6	C(40): 2.0	0.4
2019	HOU	MLB	32	98	96	.212	0.0	C(26): 0.1, 1B(1): -0.0	0.5
2019	KC	MLB	32	263	76	.270	-4.6	C(73): 1.8	0.3
2019	CHC	MLB	32	13	-25	.000	-0.1	C(4): -0.2	-0.2
2020	HOU	MLB	33	165	97	.295	-1.6	C(47): -0.4	0.2
2021 FS	HOU	MLB	34	600	75	.265	-0.8	C 5, 1B 0	1.0
2021 DC	HOU	MLB	34	346	75	.265	-0.5	C 4	0.7

Martín Maldonado, continued

Batted Ball Distribution

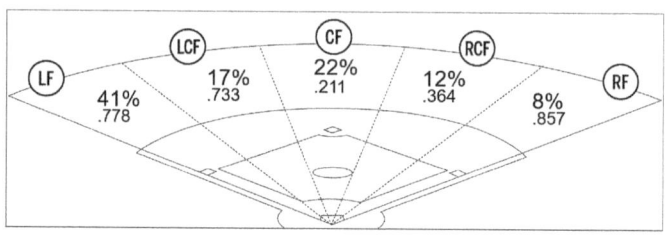

Strike Zone vs LHP   Strike Zone vs RHP

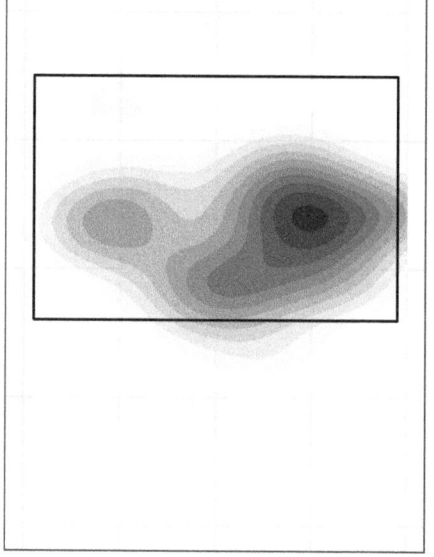

Josh Reddick RF

Born: 02/19/87 Age: 34 Bats: L Throws: R
Height: 6'2" Weight: 197 Origin: Round 17, 2006 Draft (#523 overall)

YEAR	TEAM	LVL	AGE	PA	R	2B	3B	HR	RBI	BB	K	SB	CS	AVG/OBP/SLG
2018	HOU	MLB	31	487	63	13	2	17	47	49	77	7	2	.242/.318/.400
2019	HOU	MLB	32	550	57	19	3	14	56	36	66	5	2	.275/.319/.409
2020	HOU	MLB	33	210	22	11	1	4	23	20	42	1	0	.245/.316/.378
2021 FS	HOU	MLB	34	600	65	25	2	18	69	52	111	7	4	.256/.324/.410

Comparables: Dan Ford, Alex Rios, Michael Cuddyer

Faithfully adhering to the aging curve brought Reddick great success. There were the tremendously productive years in Oakland from his mid-to-late 20s, and an extension of the peak with his excellent debut in Houston, followed by two more perfectly solid early-30s efforts. That slope proved more hazardous in 2020 as he tumbled down to replacement level, now below-average in all facets of the game. It's time for Reddick to buck the trend if he wants to continue his career, as the next point on this graph puts him beneath the threshold for a major-league roster spot.

YEAR	TEAM	LVL	AGE	PA	DRC+	BABIP	BRR	FRAA	WARP
2018	HOU	MLB	31	487	105	.258	-1.0	RF(111): -2.0, LF(43): 0.4	1.2
2019	HOU	MLB	32	550	97	.288	-2.2	RF(119): 5.2, LF(29): -1.1, CF(9): -0.4	1.3
2020	HOU	MLB	33	210	94	.294	-0.9	RF(50): 0.7	0.2
2021 FS	HOU	MLB	34	600	97	.294	0.0	RF 2, LF 0	1.2

Josh Reddick, continued

Batted Ball Distribution

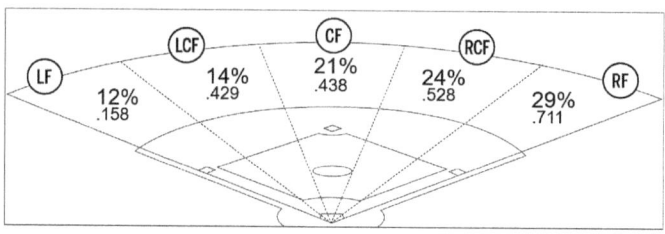

| | Strike Zone vs LHP | Strike Zone vs RHP |

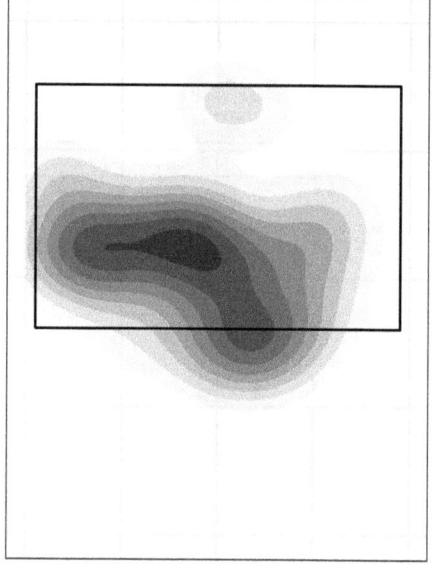

Abraham Toro 3B

Born: 12/20/96   Age: 24   Bats: S   Throws: R
Height: 6'0"   Weight: 206   Origin: Round 5, 2016 Draft (#157 overall)

YEAR	TEAM	LVL	AGE	PA	R	2B	3B	HR	RBI	BB	K	SB	CS	AVG/OBP/SLG
2018	FAY	HI-A	21	349	54	20	1	14	56	45	62	5	1	.257/.361/.473
2018	CC	AA	21	202	16	15	2	2	22	17	46	3	3	.230/.317/.371
2019	CC	AA	22	435	65	22	4	16	70	48	77	4	1	.306/.393/.513
2019	RR	AAA	22	79	17	9	0	1	10	10	5	0	1	.424/.506/.606
2019	HOU	MLB	22	89	13	3	2	2	9	9	19	1	1	.218/.303/.385
2020	HOU	MLB	23	97	13	2	0	3	9	3	23	1	1	.149/.237/.276
2021 FS	HOU	MLB	24	600	78	24	3	23	77	46	148	2	1	.234/.311/.419
2021 DC	HOU	MLB	24	227	29	9	1	8	29	17	56	0	1	.234/.311/.419

Comparables: Josh Bell, Cody Asche, Mat Gamel

Blocked at both infield corners, Toro looked set to spend the season as a rarely-used bench bat. Injuries at both third base and DH offered him an early opportunity to show he could be more. Instead he reinforced the case for the bench role. Yuli Gurriel's extension and the lack of impact at the plate will likely condemn Toro to another backup campaign, unless he makes a transition to an outfield corner and develops the bat to go with it.

YEAR	TEAM	LVL	AGE	PA	DRC+	BABIP	BRR	FRAA	WARP
2018	FAY	HI-A	21	349	151	.278	1.7	3B(81): 3.4	2.9
2018	CC	AA	21	202	87	.298	-2.6	3B(43): -0.7	-0.5
2019	CC	AA	22	435	161	.346	-0.6	3B(85): 6.3, 2B(11): 0.2, 1B(6): 0.1	4.6
2019	RR	AAA	22	79	174	.443	1.9	3B(8): -0.7, 2B(4): -0.2, 1B(1): -0.0	1.0
2019	HOU	MLB	22	89	79	.259	-0.1	3B(24): -0.8, 1B(1): 0.0	0.0
2020	HOU	MLB	23	97	79	.164	-0.9	3B(14): -0.0, 1B(4): 0.3, 2B(1): -0.1	-0.1
2021 FS	HOU	MLB	24	600	94	.283	-0.4	3B 0, 1B 1	0.8
2021 DC	HOU	MLB	24	227	94	.283	-0.2	3B 0, LF 0	0.3

Abraham Toro, continued

Batted Ball Distribution

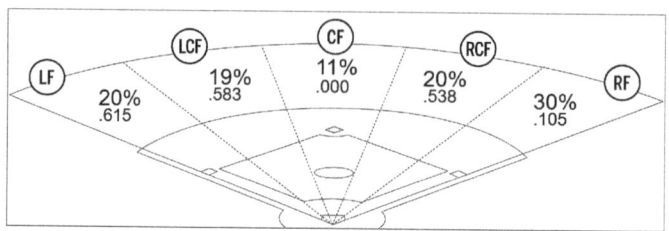

Strike Zone vs LHP   Strike Zone vs RHP

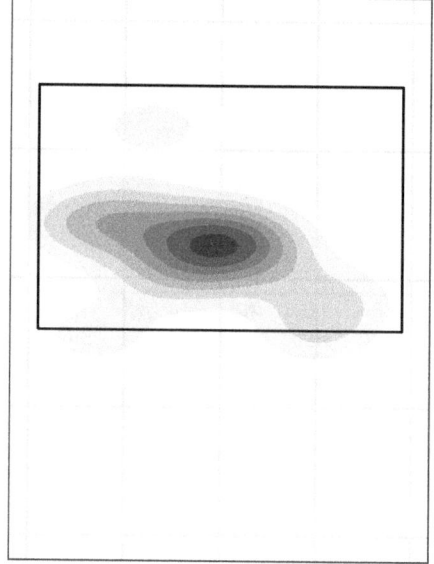

Kyle Tucker   RF

Born: 01/17/97   Age: 24   Bats: L   Throws: R
Height: 6'4"   Weight: 199   Origin: Round 1, 2015 Draft (#5 overall)

YEAR	TEAM	LVL	AGE	PA	R	2B	3B	HR	RBI	BB	K	SB	CS	AVG/OBP/SLG
2018	FRE	AAA	21	465	86	27	3	24	93	48	84	20	4	.332/.400/.590
2018	HOU	MLB	21	72	10	2	1	0	4	6	13	1	1	.141/.236/.203
2019	RR	AAA	22	536	92	26	3	34	97	60	116	30	5	.266/.354/.555
2019	HOU	MLB	22	72	15	6	0	4	11	4	20	5	0	.269/.319/.537
2020	HOU	MLB	23	228	33	12	6	9	42	18	46	8	1	.268/.325/.512
2021 FS	HOU	MLB	24	600	89	30	5	32	97	49	135	12	5	.263/.333/.514
2021 DC	HOU	MLB	24	581	86	29	4	31	94	47	131	12	5	.263/.333/.514

Comparables: Luis Gonzalez, Alex Johnson, Mel Hall

Tucker's prospect standing long appeared at odds with Houston's reticence to hand him a starting role. The team continued to insist that Josh Reddick would start over Tucker right up until the much-delayed Opening Day, when Yordan Alvarez's absence left a void in the lineup. Tucker showed he could hold his own and laced a league-leading triple total, but he fell a little short of the truly explosive offensive performance that he produced in the minors. He was still one of the biggest offensive threats on a disappointing Houston offense, and his starting role is not under threat regardless. Free agency severely depleted the established outfield, leaving Tucker, at just 24, as the presumptive cornerstone for the next half-decade.

YEAR	TEAM	LVL	AGE	PA	DRC+	BABIP	BRR	FRAA	WARP
2018	FRE	AAA	21	465	160	.364	1.7	RF(54): 0.3, LF(32): -0.4, CF(4): -0.4	3.6
2018	HOU	MLB	21	72	72	.176	-0.4	LF(20): -2.1, RF(3): 0.2, CF(1): -0.0	-0.3
2019	RR	AAA	22	536	114	.280	1.3	RF(60): 3.2, LF(40): -0.3, 1B(11): 0.3	2.4
2019	HOU	MLB	22	72	87	.326	0.6	LF(11): -0.4, RF(11): 0.9, 1B(4): 0.0	0.2
2020	HOU	MLB	23	228	116	.303	0.2	LF(41): 3.1, RF(7): 0.5	1.4
2021 FS	HOU	MLB	24	600	118	.300	1.1	RF 5, CF -1	3.3
2021 DC	HOU	MLB	24	581	118	.300	1.0	RF 5, CF -1	3.2

Kyle Tucker, continued

Batted Ball Distribution

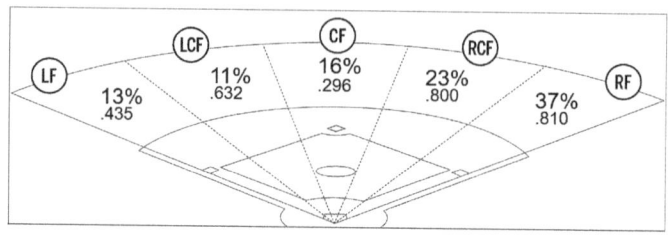

Strike Zone vs LHP   **Strike Zone vs RHP**

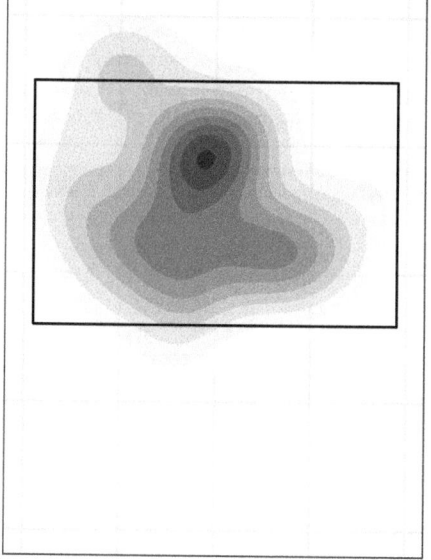

Pedro Báez RHP

Born: 03/11/88 Age: 33 Bats: R Throws: R
Height: 6'0" Weight: 232 Origin: International Free Agent, 2007

YEAR	TEAM	LVL	AGE	W	L	SV	G	GS	IP	H	HR	BB/9	K/9	K	GB%	BABIP
2018	LAD	MLB	30	4	3	0	55	0	56^1	46	4	3.7	9.9	62	35.1%	.290
2019	LAD	MLB	31	7	2	1	71	0	69^2	43	6	3.0	8.9	69	35.6%	.215
2020	LAD	MLB	32	0	0	2	18	0	17	10	2	3.7	6.9	13	36.0%	.167
2021 FS	HOU	MLB	33	2	2	2	57	0	50	42	7	3.6	8.9	49	36.9%	.270
2021 DC	HOU	MLB	33	3	3	2	65	0	56	48	8	3.6	8.9	55	36.9%	.270

Comparables: Hector Rondón, Bryan Shaw, Shawn Kelley

For years, Báez has been infamous for working slowly. Quietly though, he's done us all the favor of keeping at-bats relatively short, which kept his appearances from being as soporific as they might have been. The proof of that came in 2020, when he lost 1.5 mph on his fastball, used his slider and changeup more to try to cover for it, threw 4.37 pitches per plate appearance and became fully unwatchable. (Also, despite a fine ERA, he was quite a bit worse.)

YEAR	TEAM	LVL	AGE	WHIP	ERA	DRA-	WARP	MPH	FB%	WHF	CSP
2018	LAD	MLB	30	1.22	2.88	74	1.0	97.6	62.8%	31.3%	
2019	LAD	MLB	31	0.95	3.10	75	1.3	97.4	50.7%	31.8%	
2020	LAD	MLB	32	1.00	3.18	112	0.0	95.6	42.2%	28.8%	
2021 FS	HOU	MLB	33	1.26	3.73	85	0.6	97.0	51.6%	31.0%	42.6%
2021 DC	HOU	MLB	33	1.26	3.73	85	0.7	97.0	51.6%	31.0%	42.6%

Houston Astros 2021

Pedro Báez, continued

Pitch Shape vs LHH

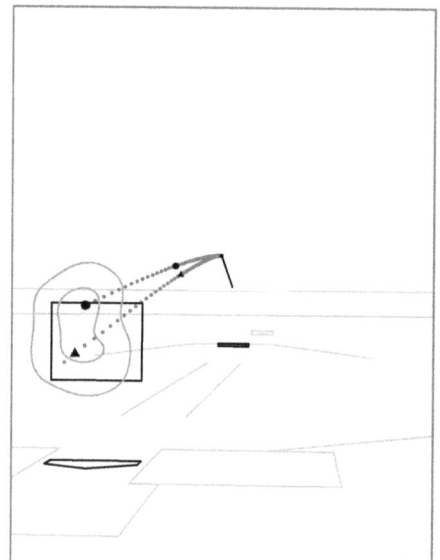

Pitch Shape vs RHH

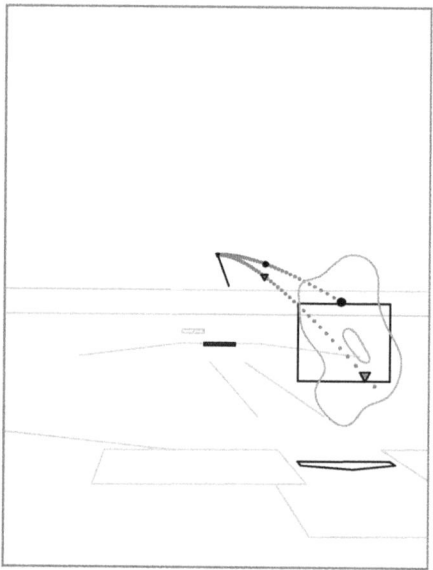

Type	Frequency	Velocity	H Movement	V Movement
● Fastball	42.2%	94.4 [106]	-5.1 [107]	-11.7 [110]
▲ Changeup	35.9%	86.8 [106]	-11.4 [102]	-20.9 [118]
▽ Slider	21.9%	87.1 [114]	1.7 [86]	-27.4 [118]

Brandon Bielak RHP

Born: 04/02/96   Age: 25   Bats: L   Throws: R
Height: 6'2"   Weight: 208   Origin: Round 11, 2017 Draft (#331 overall)

YEAR	TEAM	LVL	AGE	W	L	SV	G	GS	IP	H	HR	BB/9	K/9	K	GB%	BABIP
2018	FAY	HI-A	22	5	3	2	14	7	55^2	44	2	2.7	12.0	74	41.9%	.331
2018	CC	AA	22	2	5	0	11	10	61^1	52	4	3.2	8.4	57	50.3%	.296
2019	CC	AA	23	3	0	0	8	6	36	29	3	3.5	8.2	33	53.0%	.268
2019	RR	AAA	23	8	4	0	15	14	85^2	69	10	3.8	9.0	86	42.8%	.271
2020	HOU	MLB	24	3	3	0	12	6	32	39	9	4.8	7.3	26	35.9%	.323
2021 FS	HOU	MLB	25	2	3	0	57	0	50	48	9	4.4	8.3	46	41.1%	.291
2021 DC	HOU	MLB	25	3	2	0	17	6	45.3	44	8	4.4	8.3	41	41.1%	.291

Comparables: Ryan Helsley, Carlos Rosa, Kyle Wright

A strike-thrower all the way through the minors, Bielak couldn't find the balance against baseball's best. His fastball was crushed when he threw it in the zone, and he couldn't spot it effectively enough to make his secondaries play up. Nibbling around the edges only led to more walks. Bielak has to walk a tightrope if he's to stick as a fifth starter. Wobbles like this will quickly consign him to a role as a safety net.

YEAR	TEAM	LVL	AGE	WHIP	ERA	DRA-	WARP	MPH	FB%	WHF	CSP
2018	FAY	HI-A	22	1.10	2.10	52	1.8				
2018	CC	AA	22	1.21	2.35	83	0.9				
2019	CC	AA	23	1.19	3.75	82	0.4				
2019	RR	AAA	23	1.23	4.41	56	3.3				
2020	HOU	MLB	24	1.75	6.75	161	-0.8	94.5	63.8%	27.5%	
2021 FS	HOU	MLB	25	1.47	4.93	106	0.1	94.5	63.8%	27.5%	44.6%
2021 DC	HOU	MLB	25	1.47	4.93	106	0.2	94.5	63.8%	27.5%	44.6%

Brandon Bielak, continued

Pitch Shape vs LHH

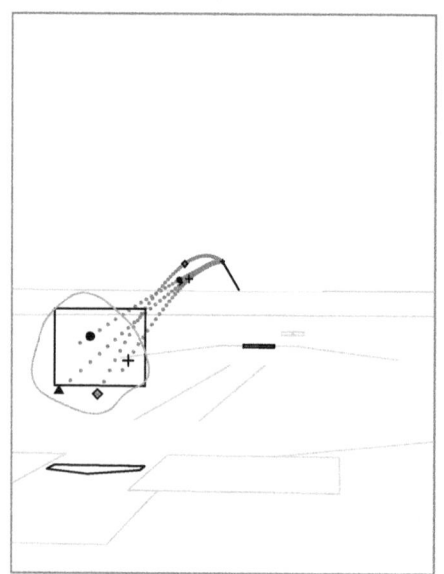

Pitch Shape vs RHH

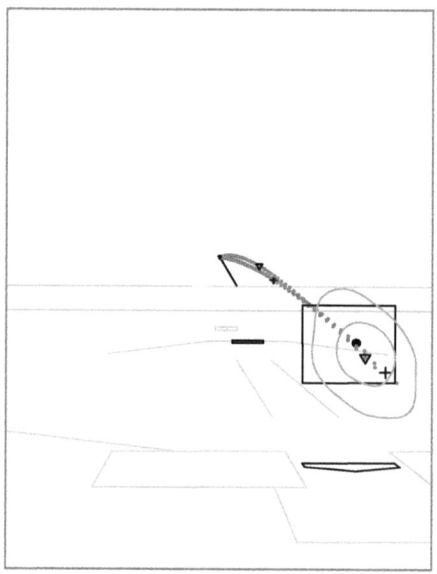

Type	Frequency	Velocity	H Movement	V Movement
● Fastball	49.4%	93.3 [102]	-7.6 [96]	-13.9 [104]
+ Cutter	14.2%	88.8 [103]	3.3 [109]	-24.9 [97]
▲ Changeup	17.4%	86.5 [105]	-14.5 [85]	-27.1 [101]
▽ Slider	10.4%	83.3 [97]	7.7 [109]	-35.1 [96]
◇ Curveball	8.4%	79.8 [104]	5.8 [93]	-53.4 [89]

Steve Cishek RHP

Born: 06/18/86 Age: 35 Bats: R Throws: R
Height: 6'6" Weight: 215 Origin: Round 5, 2007 Draft (#166 overall)

YEAR	TEAM	LVL	AGE	W	L	SV	G	GS	IP	H	HR	BB/9	K/9	K	GB%	BABIP
2018	CHC	MLB	32	4	3	4	80	0	70^1	45	5	3.6	10.0	78	46.8%	.241
2019	CHC	MLB	33	4	6	7	70	0	64	48	7	4.1	8.0	57	49.4%	.246
2020	CHW	MLB	34	0	0	0	22	0	20	21	4	4.0	9.4	21	32.2%	.309
2021 FS	HOU	MLB	35	2	2	0	57	0	50	46	6	3.8	8.7	48	43.2%	.288

Comparables: Brad Brach, Tyler Clippard, Pedro Strop

Society is crumbling, the oceans are boiling, the West Coast is burning, and by the time this book is published, everything will be unfathomably worse than when this was written. And as we fall to our knees in torment, searching for answers on how it all got this bad and how many warning signs were missed, know that by July of 2020, an unflinching indicator that humanity was irreparably broken had already appeared. For that is when Steve Cishek, side-arming, slider-slinging right-hander of 11 major league seasons, lost the ability to get right-handers out. Dingers fly, and chaos reigns.

YEAR	TEAM	LVL	AGE	WHIP	ERA	DRA-	WARP	MPH	FB%	WHF	CSP
2018	CHC	MLB	32	1.04	2.18	104	0.2	92.3	62.3%	29.4%	
2019	CHC	MLB	33	1.20	2.95	83	0.9	92.5	59.2%	22.5%	
2020	CHW	MLB	34	1.50	5.40	121	0.0	92.5	47.6%	27.2%	
2021 FS	HOU	MLB	35	1.35	4.27	98	0.3	92.4	57.1%	25.5%	45.4%

Houston Astros 2021

Steve Cishek, continued

Pitch Shape vs LHH **Pitch Shape vs RHH**

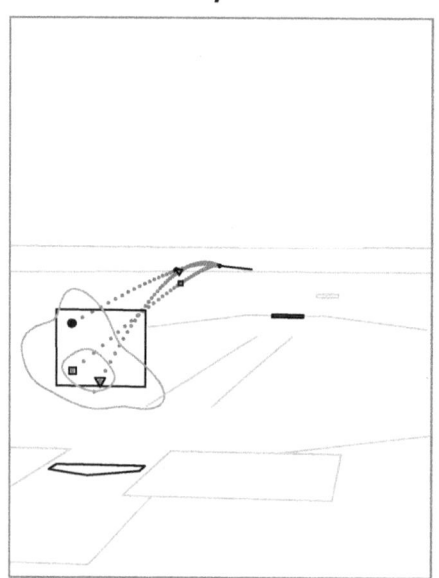 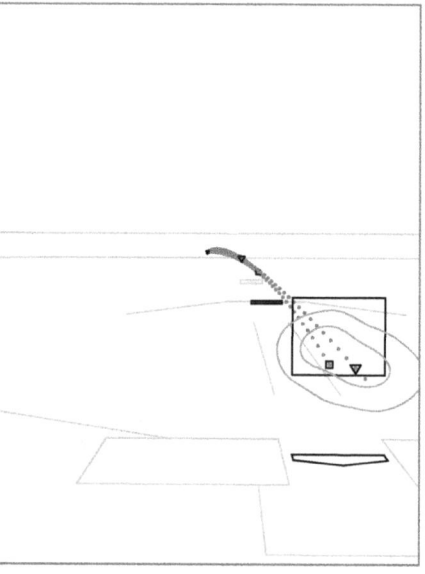

Type	Frequency	Velocity	H Movement	V Movement
● Fastball	15.5%	90.3 [93]	-9.6 [86]	-21.3 [83]
☐ Sinker	32.1%	90.7 [91]	-14.8 [87]	-25.6 [84]
▽ Slider	51.3%	78.4 [75]	11.6 [124]	-42.3 [75]

Luis Garcia RHP

Born: 12/13/96 Age: 24 Bats: R Throws: R
Height: 6'1" Weight: 244 Origin: International Free Agent, 2017

YEAR	TEAM	LVL	AGE	W	L	SV	G	GS	IP	H	HR	BB/9	K/9	K	GB%	BABIP
2018	TRI	SS	21	0	0	0	5	3	16¹	7	0	4.4	15.4	28	43.3%	.233
2018	QC	LO-A	21	7	2	0	19	10	69	58	4	4.3	9.1	70	37.3%	.300
2019	QC	LO-A	22	4	0	1	9	6	43	23	4	3.3	12.6	60	41.1%	.221
2019	FAY	HI-A	22	6	4	0	15	12	65²	43	5	4.7	14.8	108	45.3%	.311
2020	HOU	MLB	23	0	1	0	5	1	12¹	7	1	3.6	6.6	9	41.2%	.182
2021 FS	*HOU*	*MLB*	*24*	*2*	*2*	*0*	*57*	*0*	*50*	*43*	*8*	*5.3*	*10.1*	*56*	*40.6%*	*.289*
2021 DC	*HOU*	*MLB*	*24*	*0*	*0*	*0*	*3*	*3*	*13.7*	*12*	*2*	*5.3*	*10.1*	*15*	*40.6%*	*.289*

Comparables: Vince Velasquez, Jorge Alcala, Cristian Javier

This Luis Garcia might be the worst-ranked and least-known of the current batch of prospects with the same name, but he made the jump from High-A to the majors without looking overmatched. His five-pitch mix includes a changeup and slider that both drew whiffs from big-league hitters. If his command can come around enough to earn a spot in the rotation, Garcia might yet be able to climb the Luis Garcia Power Rankings, although he'll have a hard time topping the version starting on the dirt for the Nationals at the age of 20.

YEAR	TEAM	LVL	AGE	WHIP	ERA	DRA-	WARP	MPH	FB%	WHF	CSP
2018	TRI	SS	21	0.92	0.00	237	-1.1				
2018	QC	LO-A	21	1.32	2.48	74	1.3				
2019	QC	LO-A	22	0.91	2.93	55	1.2				
2019	FAY	HI-A	22	1.17	3.02	66	1.4				
2020	HOU	MLB	23	0.97	2.92	110	0.0	96.0	59.1%	26.1%	
2021 FS	*HOU*	*MLB*	*24*	*1.47*	*4.64*	*101*	*0.2*	*96.0*	*59.1%*	*26.1%*	*45.2%*
2021 DC	*HOU*	*MLB*	*24*	*1.47*	*4.64*	*101*	*0.1*	*96.0*	*59.1%*	*26.1%*	*45.2%*

Luis Garcia, continued

Pitch Shape vs LHH

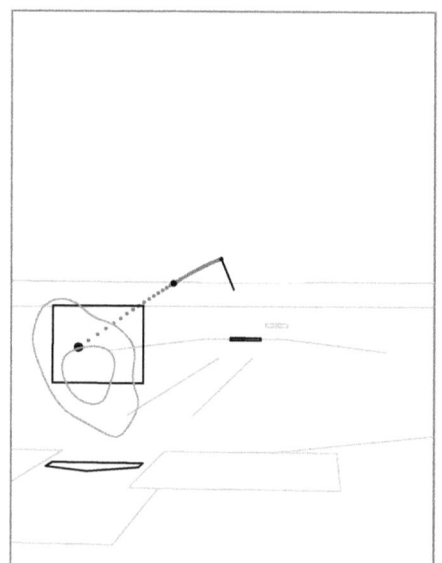

Pitch Shape vs RHH

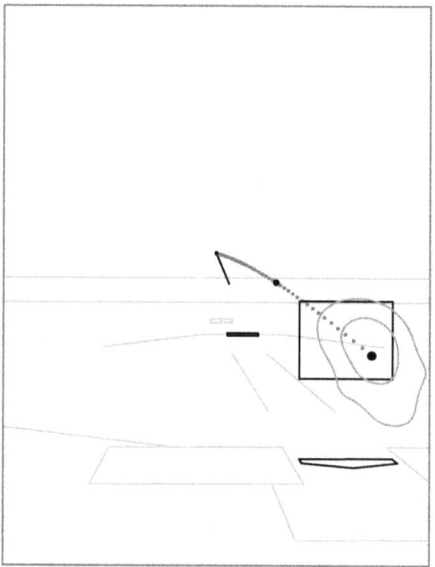

Type	Frequency	Velocity	H Movement	V Movement
● Fastball	53.7%	94.1 [105]	-5.9 [104]	-12 [109]
+ Cutter	5.4%	87.5 [95]	1.1 [95]	-25.3 [96]
▲ Changeup	18.2%	82.8 [91]	-15.2 [82]	-29.7 [94]
▽ Slider	15.3%	81.4 [89]	10.7 [121]	-39.1 [84]
◇ Curveball	7.4%	76.8 [93]	7.7 [101]	-54.3 [87]

Zack Greinke RHP

Born: 10/21/83 Age: 37 Bats: R Throws: R
Height: 6'2" Weight: 200 Origin: Round 1, 2002 Draft (#6 overall)

YEAR	TEAM	LVL	AGE	W	L	SV	G	GS	IP	H	HR	BB/9	K/9	K	GB%	BABIP
2018	ARI	MLB	34	15	11	0	33	33	207^2	181	28	1.9	8.6	199	44.8%	.273
2019	ARI	MLB	35	10	4	0	23	23	146	117	15	1.3	8.3	135	41.9%	.266
2019	HOU	MLB	35	8	1	0	10	10	62^2	58	6	1.3	7.5	52	51.1%	.291
2020	HOU	MLB	36	3	3	0	12	12	67	67	6	1.2	9.0	67	41.8%	.321
2021 FS	HOU	MLB	37	10	7	0	26	26	150	140	24	1.8	8.4	140	43.6%	.287
2021 DC	HOU	MLB	37	12	8	0	30	30	184.7	173	29	1.8	8.4	172	43.6%	.287

Comparables: Mike Mussina, Justin Verlander, Fergie Jenkins

Greinke produced a striking portfolio of moments that defined both his incomparable career and the entire 2020 season. There was his decision to take his seat with a group of cardboard cutouts on August 7, an effort at more effective social distancing given the limitations of dugouts. That was followed by a duo of iconic Greinke incidents on August 23. An inning after he had thrown a 54 mph eephus for a strike—a pitchout attempt gone awry in a manner only he could conjure—the 17-year veteran was unhappy with the condition of the mound. Upon calling out the groundskeepers to fix it, Greinke sat down on the grass, a cross-legged Zen-like figure waiting for the issue to be resolved. There's more: a whole essay could be devoted to the topic of if or when he was calling his own pitches from the mound. Amidst all the chaos, there was something calming about Greinke going about his business in a typically unconventional manner. The most comforting aspect of all was his reaction to our fascination with his antics, treating them as if they were disappointingly mundane rather than moments that could only come from one man.

YEAR	TEAM	LVL	AGE	WHIP	ERA	DRA-	WARP	MPH	FB%	WHF	CSP
2018	ARI	MLB	34	1.08	3.21	68	5.3	91.4	48.7%	25.9%	
2019	ARI	MLB	35	0.95	2.90	62	4.3	91.7	47.7%	23.4%	
2019	HOU	MLB	35	1.07	3.02	71	1.5	92.1	43.1%	26.0%	
2020	HOU	MLB	36	1.13	4.03	81	1.3	90.0	42.4%	27.8%	
2021 FS	HOU	MLB	37	1.14	3.37	80	3.1	91.3	45.9%	25.5%	46.3%
2021 DC	HOU	MLB	37	1.14	3.37	80	3.8	91.3	45.9%	25.5%	46.3%

Houston Astros 2021

Zack Greinke, continued

Pitch Shape vs LHH
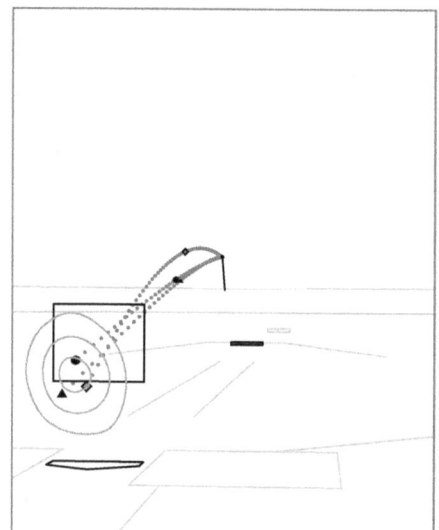

Pitch Shape vs RHH
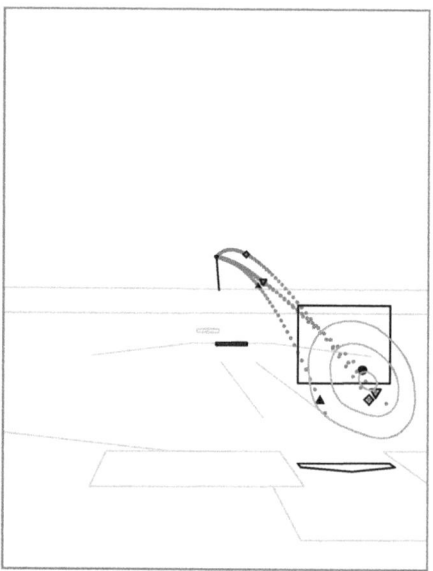

Type	Frequency	Velocity	H Movement	V Movement
● Fastball	42.1%	88 [85]	-1 [127]	-16.3 [97]
▲ Changeup	22.6%	86 [103]	-11.7 [100]	-29.3 [95]
▽ Slider	16.2%	84.6 [103]	5.8 [102]	-29.1 [113]
◇ Curveball	15.0%	70.7 [69]	9.6 [108]	-59.8 [74]

Josh James RHP

Born: 03/08/93   Age: 28   Bats: R   Throws: R
Height: 6'3"   Weight: 234   Origin: Round 34, 2014 Draft (#1006 overall)

YEAR	TEAM	LVL	AGE	W	L	SV	G	GS	IP	H	HR	BB/9	K/9	K	GB%	BABIP
2018	CC	AA	25	0	0	1	6	4	21^2	17	1	4.2	15.8	38	57.8%	.364
2018	FRE	AAA	25	6	4	0	17	17	92^2	62	8	3.8	12.9	133	39.6%	.280
2018	HOU	MLB	25	2	0	0	6	3	23	15	3	2.7	11.3	29	41.5%	.240
2019	HOU	MLB	26	5	1	1	49	1	61^1	46	10	5.1	14.7	100	35.4%	.308
2020	HOU	MLB	27	1	0	0	13	2	17^1	15	4	8.8	10.9	21	32.6%	.282
2021 FS	*HOU*	*MLB*	*28*	*2*	*2*	*0*	*57*	*0*	*50*	*40*	*8*	*5.1*	*11.7*	*65*	*38.1%*	*.290*
2021 DC	*HOU*	*MLB*	*28*	*2*	*2*	*0*	*17*	*6*	*37*	*30*	*6*	*5.1*	*11.7*	*48*	*38.1%*	*.290*

Comparables: Erick Fedde, Scott Barlow, Ryne Stanek

A major-league baseball field: one of the most hostile places on Earth. This young right-handed pitcher fights to survive in a system that can sustain only a limited amount of his kind. His arm is his weapon, capable of launching projectiles at 100 miles per hour. It's an exceptional physical feat. His prey can be struck down before they have time to react—if he gets it right.

This is not only a case of raw strength. Extraordinary coordination is required too. Not all learn it. This youngster is not at full health, and is wild. Too wild, and he misses the target. Now the hunter becomes the hunted, foe primed to counterattack. The pitcher flees, hoping to fight again another day. He might have escaped this time, but he's still in peril. There will be others waiting to take his place if he does not learn how to thrive.

YEAR	TEAM	LVL	AGE	WHIP	ERA	DRA-	WARP	MPH	FB%	WHF	CSP
2018	CC	AA	25	1.25	2.49	35	0.9				
2018	FRE	AAA	25	1.09	3.40	50	3.3				
2018	HOU	MLB	25	0.96	2.35	71	0.5	99.9	59.9%	31.1%	
2019	HOU	MLB	26	1.32	4.70	68	1.3	99.3	63.3%	36.7%	
2020	HOU	MLB	27	1.85	7.27	137	-0.2	98.5	57.8%	30.6%	
2021 FS	*HOU*	*MLB*	*28*	*1.38*	*4.29*	*94*	*0.4*	*99.2*	*61.5%*	*34.5%*	*45.6%*
2021 DC	*HOU*	*MLB*	*28*	*1.38*	*4.29*	*94*	*0.4*	*99.2*	*61.5%*	*34.5%*	*45.6%*

Josh James, continued

Pitch Shape vs LHH

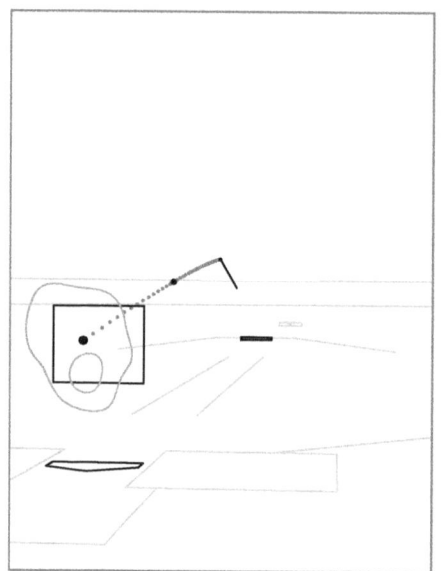

Pitch Shape vs RHH

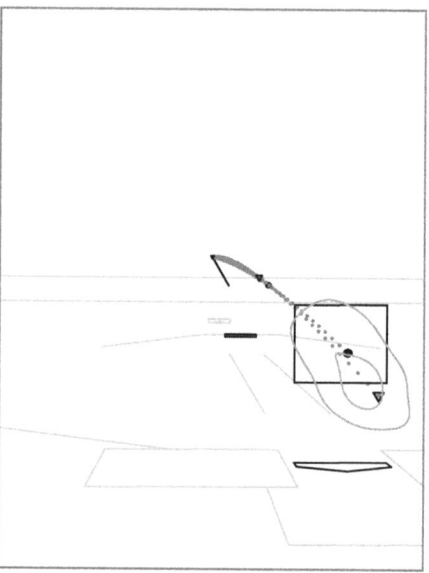

Type	Frequency	Velocity	H Movement	V Movement
● Fastball	57.6%	96.4 [112]	-7.2 [98]	-12.6 [107]
▲ Changeup	13.5%	88.9 [115]	-13.9 [89]	-28.9 [96]
▽ Slider	23.8%	85.7 [108]	8.3 [111]	-35.6 [95]
◇ Curveball	4.7%	82.4 [115]	4.7 [89]	-49.5 [97]

Cristian Javier   RHP

Born: 03/26/97   Age: 24   Bats: R   Throws: R
Height: 6'1"   Weight: 213   Origin: International Free Agent, 2015

YEAR	TEAM	LVL	AGE	W	L	SV	G	GS	IP	H	HR	BB/9	K/9	K	GB%	BABIP
2018	QC	LO-A	21	2	2	1	11	7	49^1	28	3	4.2	14.6	80	30.4%	.281
2018	FAY	HI-A	21	5	4	0	14	11	60^2	44	6	4.0	9.8	66	31.8%	.257
2019	FAY	HI-A	22	2	0	1	7	5	28^2	15	1	5.0	12.6	40	33.3%	.226
2019	CC	AA	22	6	3	3	17	11	74	31	5	4.7	13.9	114	29.2%	.198
2019	RR	AAA	22	0	0	0	2	2	11	5	1	3.3	13.1	16	17.4%	.182
2020	HOU	MLB	23	5	2	0	12	10	54^1	36	11	3.0	8.9	54	29.3%	.194
2021 FS	HOU	MLB	24	9	8	0	26	26	150	130	30	4.6	10.7	178	30.2%	.283
2021 DC	HOU	MLB	24	7	7	0	22	22	113.3	98	22	4.6	10.7	134	30.2%	.283

Comparables: Jorge Alcala, Mitch Keller, Carlos Rodón

Javier bailed out an Astros staff that desperately needed pitching help, weaving the latest strand of a relentlessly successful pro career. His four-seamer might have below-average velocity, but it tied most hitters down with pop-ups and weak fly balls. While a few too many of those flies escaped the field of play, Javier kept the numbers on base under wraps via a sweeping slider that generated whiffs on 57 percent of swings. A more reliable third pitch would secure his spot in the rotation. There's already enough here to leave hitters' heads spinning in shorter stints.

YEAR	TEAM	LVL	AGE	WHIP	ERA	DRA-	WARP	MPH	FB%	WHF	CSP
2018	QC	LO-A	21	1.03	1.82	42	1.8				
2018	FAY	HI-A	21	1.17	3.41	69	1.4				
2019	FAY	HI-A	22	1.08	0.94	59	0.7				
2019	CC	AA	22	0.95	2.07	43	2.5				
2019	RR	AAA	22	0.82	1.64	54	0.4				
2020	HOU	MLB	23	0.99	3.48	128	-0.3	94.2	63.1%	22.5%	
2021 FS	HOU	MLB	24	1.38	4.59	100	1.4	94.2	63.1%	22.5%	48.1%
2021 DC	HOU	MLB	24	1.38	4.59	100	1.1	94.2	63.1%	22.5%	48.1%

Cristian Javier, continued

Pitch Shape vs LHH

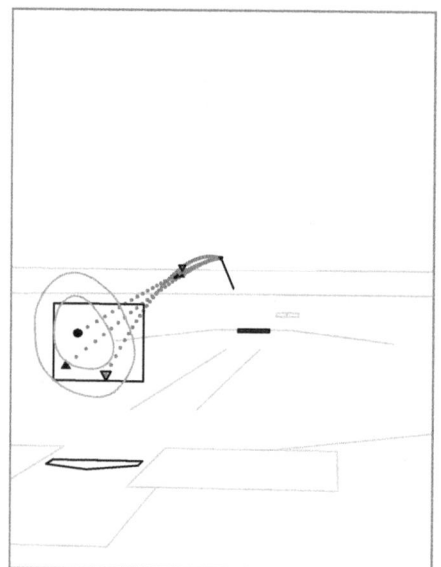

Pitch Shape vs RHH

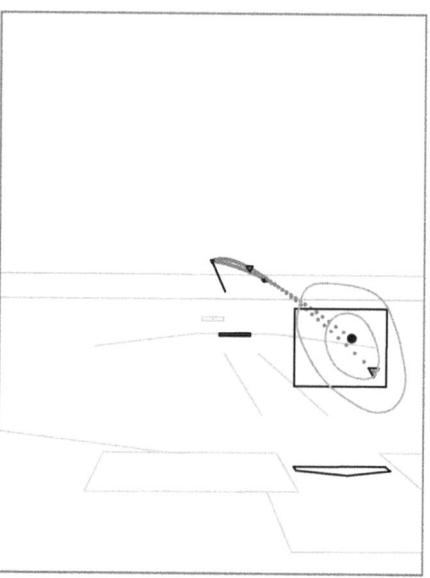

Type	Frequency	Velocity	H Movement	V Movement
● Fastball	63.0%	92.3 [99]	-6.3 [102]	-12.8 [107]
▲ Changeup	7.2%	86 [103]	-14.4 [86]	-25.4 [106]
▽ Slider	26.2%	78.8 [77]	11.3 [123]	-37.3 [90]
◇ Curveball	3.5%	76.3 [91]	10.5 [112]	-51.7 [93]

Lance McCullers Jr. RHP

Born: 10/02/93 Age: 27 Bats: L Throws: R
Height: 6'1" Weight: 202 Origin: Round 1, 2012 Draft (#41 overall)

YEAR	TEAM	LVL	AGE	W	L	SV	G	GS	IP	H	HR	BB/9	K/9	K	GB%	BABIP
2018	HOU	MLB	24	10	6	0	25	22	128^1	100	12	3.5	10.0	142	54.9%	.279
2020	HOU	MLB	26	3	3	0	11	11	55	44	5	3.3	9.2	56	58.9%	.279
2021 FS	HOU	MLB	27	10	7	0	26	26	150	130	17	4.2	10.1	169	55.4%	.297
2021 DC	HOU	MLB	27	9	7	0	25	25	137.3	119	16	4.2	10.1	154	55.4%	.297

Comparables: Yovani Gallardo, Luis Castillo, Scott Kazmir

McCullers made a largely successful return from Tommy John surgery, albeit with some diminished velocity. It wasn't his high heat that was affected so much as his curveball, however. Its descent into the low-80s band added a little more drop, but also some extra-base hits. Opposing hitters slugged .481 against the pitch and appeared to adopt an all-or-nothing approach once the playoffs rolled around. McCullers served up seven dingers in total across three postseason starts, including three off the curve, while also punching out 23 in 14 2/3 frames. The results on the breaker, both in reality and expected, have been slowly but steadily getting worse since 2016. McCullers can get by just fine if he halts the decline here, but it's no longer a pitch that would get thrown 24 times in a row or feature on the cover of *Sports Illustrated*.

YEAR	TEAM	LVL	AGE	WHIP	ERA	DRA-	WARP	MPH	FB%	WHF	CSP
2018	HOU	MLB	24	1.17	3.86	73	3.0	96.3	37.3%	31.6%	
2020	HOU	MLB	26	1.16	3.93	78	1.1	96.0	44.1%	29.7%	
2021 FS	HOU	MLB	27	1.33	3.80	87	2.5	96.1	41.1%	30.5%	43.9%
2021 DC	HOU	MLB	27	1.33	3.80	87	2.3	96.1	41.1%	30.5%	43.9%

Houston Astros 2021

Lance McCullers Jr., continued

Pitch Shape vs LHH

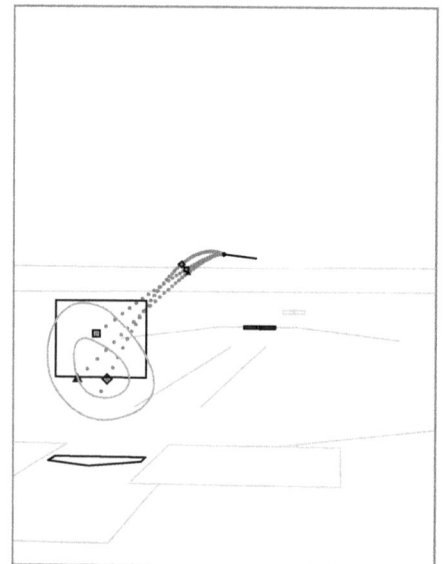

Pitch Shape vs RHH

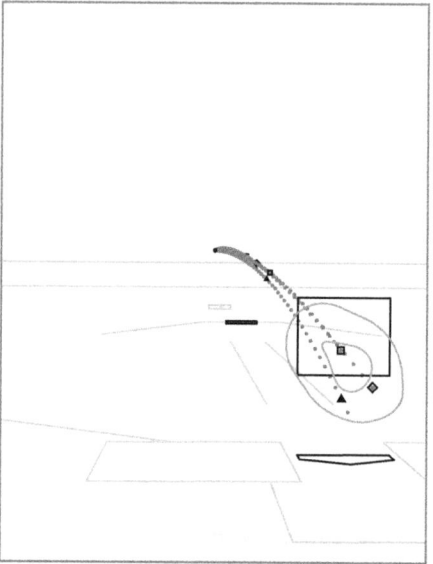

Type	Frequency	Velocity	H Movement	V Movement
☐ Sinker	41.0%	93.9 [107]	-13.4 [98]	-21.6 [96]
▲ Changeup	18.3%	86.4 [105]	-14.9 [83]	-31.8 [88]
◇ Curveball	37.6%	83.5 [119]	10.5 [112]	-45.1 [107]

Enoli Paredes   RHP

Born: 09/28/95   Age: 25   Bats: R   Throws: R
Height: 5'11"   Weight: 171   Origin: International Free Agent, 2015

YEAR	TEAM	LVL	AGE	W	L	SV	G	GS	IP	H	HR	BB/9	K/9	K	GB%	BABIP
2018	QC	LO-A	22	2	3	2	16	5	55²	28	0	4.2	11.5	71	44.9%	.220
2018	FAY	HI-A	22	4	1	0	8	0	13¹	6	1	2.0	12.8	19	32.1%	.200
2019	FAY	HI-A	23	3	1	0	10	6	44	21	3	4.3	12.1	59	44.0%	.205
2019	CC	AA	23	2	3	1	12	6	50	29	1	3.8	12.4	69	35.8%	.269
2020	HOU	MLB	24	3	3	0	22	0	20²	18	1	4.8	8.7	20	43.1%	.304
2021 FS	HOU	MLB	25	2	3	4	57	0	50	45	8	5.3	10.3	57	39.9%	.300
2021 DC	HOU	MLB	25	2	2	4	53	0	56	51	9	5.3	10.3	64	39.9%	.300

Comparables: Freddy Peralta, Adonis Rosa, David Bednar

Paredes rapidly flattens his body out and then explodes back to his full height during his delivery, a process that often finishes with a jaunty hop as the pitch crosses the plate. It's the product of a huge stride that helps to propel his high-90s fastball from a relatively compact frame and puts his release point about as low as it's possible to get without being labeled a side-armer. When Paredes locates the heater up in the zone, the plane is consequently so flat that hitters have real trouble getting the barrel to the ball. In the lower regions, it's not so effective. His command needs some work if he's going to hit those more favorable spots consistently. No matter where the pitch is located, having the pitcher pop up off the mound like a jack-in-a-box is going to remain distracting for hitters.

YEAR	TEAM	LVL	AGE	WHIP	ERA	DRA-	WARP	MPH	FB%	WHF	CSP
2018	QC	LO-A	22	0.97	1.46	68	1.2				
2018	FAY	HI-A	22	0.68	1.35	54	0.4				
2019	FAY	HI-A	23	0.95	1.64	53	1.2				
2019	CC	AA	23	1.00	3.78	58	1.2				
2020	HOU	MLB	24	1.40	3.05	96	0.2	97.9	68.2%	32.3%	
2021 FS	HOU	MLB	25	1.50	4.93	105	0.1	97.9	68.2%	32.3%	49.6%
2021 DC	HOU	MLB	25	1.50	4.93	105	0.1	97.9	68.2%	32.3%	49.6%

Enoli Paredes, continued

Pitch Shape vs LHH

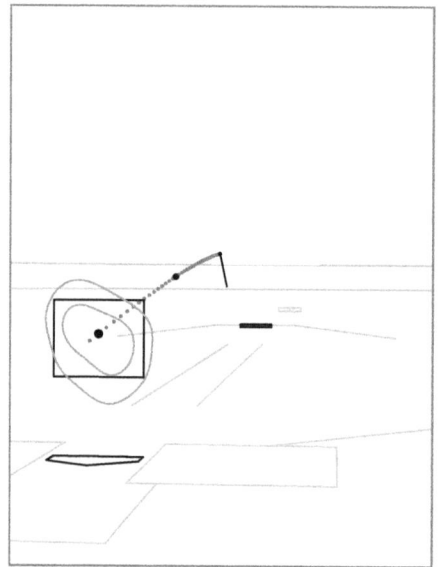

Pitch Shape vs RHH

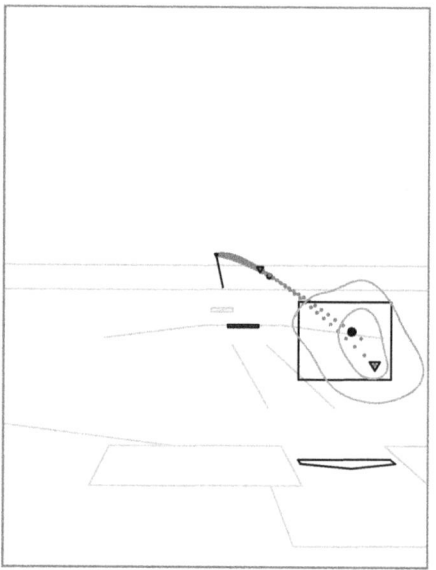

Type	Frequency	Velocity	H Movement	V Movement
● Fastball	68.2%	95.8 [110]	-2.8 [119]	-12.2 [109]
▽ Slider	26.8%	85.6 [107]	8.4 [112]	-31.5 [106]
◇ Curveball	3.0%	80.5 [107]	12.3 [119]	-46.8 [104]

Ryan Pressly RHP

Born: 12/15/88 Age: 32 Bats: R Throws: R
Height: 6'2" Weight: 206 Origin: Round 11, 2007 Draft (#354 overall)

YEAR	TEAM	LVL	AGE	W	L	SV	G	GS	IP	H	HR	BB/9	K/9	K	GB%	BABIP
2018	HOU	MLB	29	1	0	2	26	0	23^1	11	1	1.2	12.3	32	62.5%	.213
2018	MIN	MLB	29	1	1	0	51	0	47^2	46	5	3.6	13.0	69	48.3%	.366
2019	HOU	MLB	30	2	3	3	55	0	54^1	37	6	2.0	11.9	72	52.4%	.258
2020	HOU	MLB	31	1	3	12	23	0	21	21	2	3.0	12.4	29	48.1%	.365
2021 FS	HOU	MLB	32	3	2	36	57	0	50	41	6	3.2	11.2	62	47.5%	.297
2021 DC	HOU	MLB	32	2	2	36	53	0	56	46	7	3.2	11.2	70	47.5%	.297

Comparables: Alex Colomé, Bryan Shaw, Hunter Strickland

Pressly has cruised almost effortlessly through innings since Houston acquired him, so naturally his opportunity to take the helm in the ninth arrived when the situation turned stormy. Roberto Osuna's season was wrecked by UCL trouble, tossing Pressly into the closer role almost immediately upon his return from elbow discomfort of his own. The 31-year-old's velocity took a dive, and he proceeded to give up runs in back-to-back appearances for the first time since joining the team. As most of Houston's staff sank around him and a swath of rookies scrambled to plug the holes, Pressly steadied the ship and pitched to a 2.21 ERA the rest of the way, tripling his career save total in the process. As if to underline the point that he was the safest pair of hands around, he sailed through four postseason save opportunities with scoreless innings.

YEAR	TEAM	LVL	AGE	WHIP	ERA	DRA-	WARP	MPH	FB%	WHF	CSP
2018	HOU	MLB	29	0.60	0.77	38	0.9	97.4	34.7%	37.6%	
2018	MIN	MLB	29	1.36	3.40	44	1.6	97.8	48.7%	38.0%	
2019	HOU	MLB	30	0.90	2.32	53	1.6	97.2	35.7%	36.0%	
2020	HOU	MLB	31	1.33	3.43	74	0.5	96.3	37.1%	36.5%	
2021 FS	HOU	MLB	32	1.18	3.13	74	1.0	97.1	38.7%	36.7%	46.4%
2021 DC	HOU	MLB	32	1.18	3.13	74	1.1	97.1	38.7%	36.7%	46.4%

Houston Astros 2021

Ryan Pressly, continued

Pitch Shape vs LHH

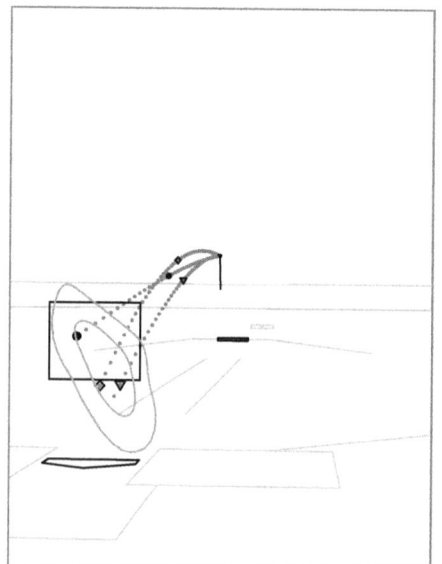

Pitch Shape vs RHH

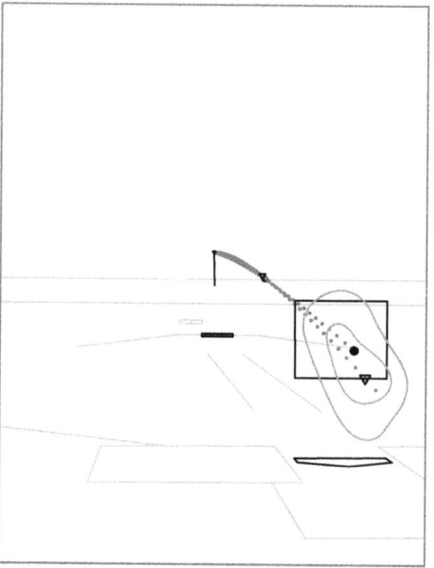

Type	Frequency	Velocity	H Movement	V Movement
● Fastball	36.7%	94.7 [107]	-0.2 [131]	-13.2 [106]
▽ Slider	41.5%	89 [122]	4.6 [97]	-29.6 [112]
◇ Curveball	20.7%	81.4 [111]	12.4 [119]	-50.9 [94]

Brooks Raley LHP

Born: 06/29/88   Age: 33   Bats: L   Throws: L
Height: 6'3"   Weight: 200   Origin: Round 6, 2009 Draft (#200 overall)

YEAR	TEAM	LVL	AGE	W	L	SV	G	GS	IP	H	HR	BB/9	K/9	K	GB%	BABIP
2020	HOU	MLB	32	0	1	1	21	0	20	13	3	2.7	12.2	27	38.3%	.233
2021 FS	HOU	MLB	33	2	2	0	57	0	50	48	8	3.9	8.4	46	40.7%	.293
2021 DC	HOU	MLB	33	2	2	0	53	0	56	54	9	3.9	8.4	52	40.7%	.293

Comparables: Chris Rusin, Héctor Noesi, Zack Britton

It may come as a surprise that Raley made more starts than all but eight major-league players from 2015-2019, not least because he hadn't been seen in the majors since 2013. The erstwhile Cubs depth option became one of the most dependable arms in the KBO for the Lotte Giants, making at least 30 starts every year with a combined 4.13 ERA over more than 900 innings. Raley could still only garner a non-roster invite to spring training and eventually got assigned to the bullpen by the Reds, who deemed him expendable after a mere four appearances. The grateful Astros saw past the ERA and velocity to the spin numbers and snapped him up. Raley immediately began to lean on his slider along with his cutter, whiffing more than a third of batters while holding those who did make contact to the lowest average exit velocity in baseball. The veteran lefty might have another five-year run left in him if these improvements hold up over a longer campaign.

YEAR	TEAM	LVL	AGE	WHIP	ERA	DRA-	WARP	MPH	FB%	WHF	CSP
2020	HOU	MLB	32	0.95	4.95	79	0.4	91.4	68.8%	31.7%	
2021 FS	HOU	MLB	33	1.40	4.74	103	0.2	91.4	68.8%	31.7%	48.6%
2021 DC	HOU	MLB	33	1.40	4.74	103	0.2	91.4	68.8%	31.7%	48.6%

Brooks Raley, continued

Pitch Shape vs LHH

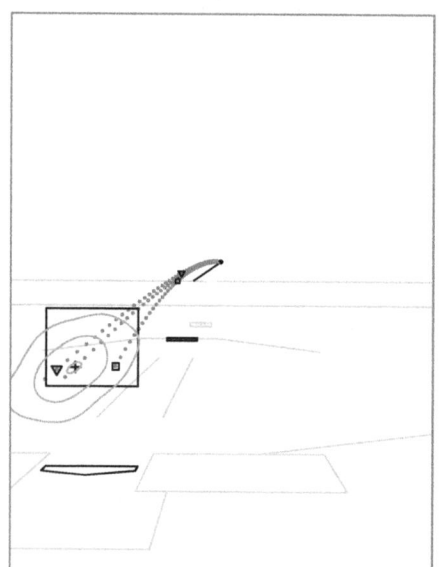

Pitch Shape vs RHH

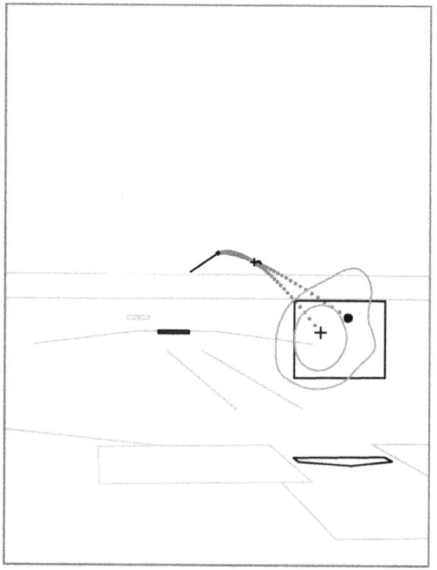

Type	Frequency	Velocity	H Movement	V Movement
● Fastball	11.3%	90.3 [93]	4.9 [109]	-17 [95]
☐ Sinker	11.6%	90.2 [89]	13.3 [98]	-23.6 [90]
+ Cutter	45.8%	86.8 [90]	-5.1 [120]	-26.8 [90]
▲ Changeup	3.6%	84.1 [96]	13 [93]	-27.1 [101]
▽ Slider	17.9%	82 [91]	-13.2 [130]	-31.9 [105]
◇ Curveball	9.8%	78.4 [99]	-14.1 [127]	-46.1 [105]

Nivaldo Rodriguez RHP

Born: 04/16/97 Age: 24 Bats: R Throws: R
Height: 6'1" Weight: 214 Origin: International Free Agent, 2016

YEAR	TEAM	LVL	AGE	W	L	SV	G	GS	IP	H	HR	BB/9	K/9	K	GB%	BABIP
2018	TRI	SS	21	4	1	1	14	7	55^2	45	3	2.1	8.1	50	42.8%	.271
2019	QC	LO-A	22	3	1	0	6	6	31	23	2	1.2	11.3	39	31.6%	.284
2019	FAY	HI-A	22	3	5	2	18	9	74	46	5	3.8	9.1	75	49.5%	.223
2020	HOU	MLB	23	0	1	0	5	0	8^2	15	3	6.2	8.3	8	43.8%	.414
2021 FS	HOU	MLB	24	2	3	0	57	0	50	49	8	4.0	8.1	45	42.7%	.294
2021 DC	HOU	MLB	24	1	1	0	21	0	22.3	22	4	4.0	8.1	20	42.7%	.294

Comparables: Bryan Abreu, Jorge Alcala, Darrell Osteen

Rodriguez was at the forefront of a glut of aggressive promotions. Events far beyond his control conspired to thrust him into the limelight almost immediately, with no minors work available and a big club that needed live arms. The challenging debut may at least make the upper minors feel more manageable when he gets an opportunity to tackle them.

YEAR	TEAM	LVL	AGE	WHIP	ERA	DRA-	WARP	MPH	FB%	WHF	CSP
2018	TRI	SS	21	1.04	2.91	260	-4.5				
2019	QC	LO-A	22	0.87	1.16	54	0.9				
2019	FAY	HI-A	22	1.04	2.92	59	1.8				
2020	HOU	MLB	23	2.42	6.23	118	0.0	94.8	49.2%	22.6%	
2021 FS	HOU	MLB	24	1.44	4.89	107	0.0	94.8	49.2%	22.6%	44.6%
2021 DC	HOU	MLB	24	1.44	4.89	107	0.0	94.8	49.2%	22.6%	44.6%

Houston Astros 2021

Nivaldo Rodriguez, continued

Pitch Shape vs LHH

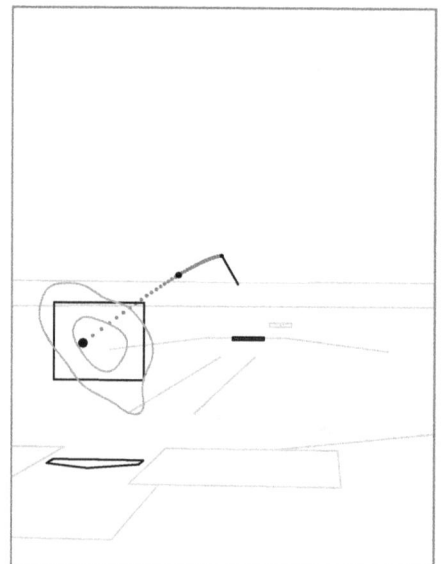

Pitch Shape vs RHH

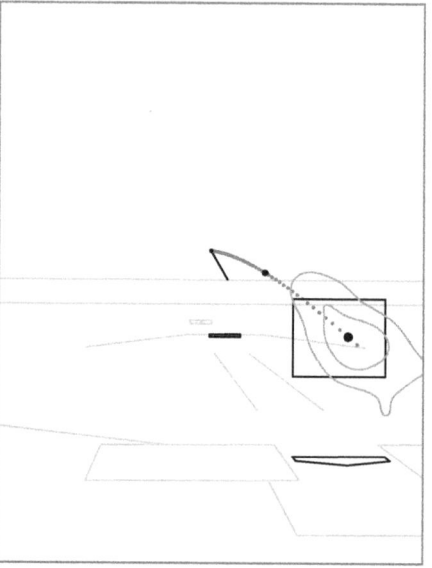

Type	Frequency	Velocity	H Movement	V Movement
● Fastball	48.2%	93 [101]	-6.5 [101]	-15.5 [99]
▲ Changeup	3.7%	83.1 [92]	-10.1 [109]	-28 [99]
▽ Slider	22.5%	89.1 [123]	2 [88]	-25.5 [124]
◇ Curveball	23.6%	83.2 [118]	4 [86]	-41.3 [116]

Andre Scrubb RHP

Born: 01/13/95 Age: 26 Bats: R Throws: R
Height: 6'4" Weight: 270 Origin: Round 8, 2016 Draft (#251 overall)

YEAR	TEAM	LVL	AGE	W	L	SV	G	GS	IP	H	HR	BB/9	K/9	K	GB%	BABIP
2018	GL	LO-A	23	3	2	2	19	0	30	33	3	4.8	10.2	34	37.6%	.366
2018	RC	HI-A	23	4	0	3	14	0	23²	8	0	4.2	10.6	28	35.2%	.148
2018	TUL	AA	23	0	0	0	5	0	9¹	6	0	4.8	9.6	10	54.2%	.250
2019	CC	AA	24	0	0	3	12	0	17	21	0	5.3	10.6	20	42.3%	.404
2019	TUL	AA	24	6	1	0	29	2	47²	35	3	4.3	10.6	56	53.7%	.276
2020	HOU	MLB	25	1	0	1	20	0	23²	15	1	7.6	9.1	24	46.6%	.250
2021 FS	HOU	MLB	26	2	3	0	57	0	50	45	6	6.6	9.5	52	46.7%	.297
2021 DC	HOU	MLB	26	2	2	0	42	0	39.3	36	5	6.6	9.5	41	46.7%	.297

Comparables: Ryan Burr, Andrew McKirahan, Scott Alexander

Circumstances conspired to send almost the entire Astros bullpen to the IL, and Scrubb was not only called into action but thrust into some high-leverage innings. His mid-90s fastball appears to be genuinely difficult to square up, helping him to overcome a walk rate that threatened to eclipse his strikeout rate. The free passes led to a few nervy innings, but ultimately Scrubb was welcome relief for a bullpen urgently in need of some TLC.

YEAR	TEAM	LVL	AGE	WHIP	ERA	DRA-	WARP	MPH	FB%	WHF	CSP
2018	GL	LO-A	23	1.63	5.10	82	0.4				
2018	RC	HI-A	23	0.80	0.38	47	0.7				
2018	TUL	AA	23	1.18	1.93	104	0.0				
2019	CC	AA	24	1.82	3.71	127	-0.3				
2019	TUL	AA	24	1.22	2.45	109	-0.4				
2020	HOU	MLB	25	1.48	1.90	98	0.2	95.1	53.1%	24.8%	
2021 FS	HOU	MLB	26	1.64	5.16	108	0.0	95.1	53.1%	24.8%	41.6%
2021 DC	HOU	MLB	26	1.64	5.16	108	0.0	95.1	53.1%	24.8%	41.6%

Houston Astros 2021

Andre Scrubb, continued

Pitch Shape vs LHH

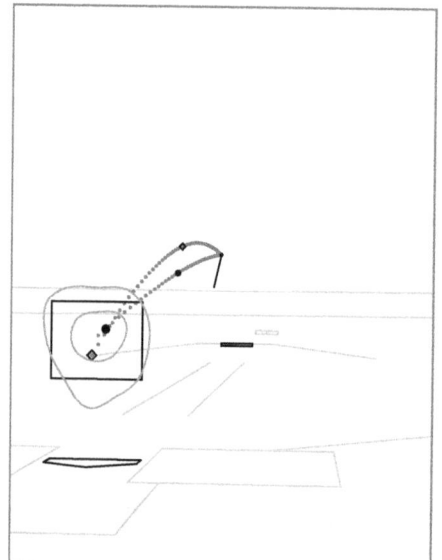

Pitch Shape vs RHH

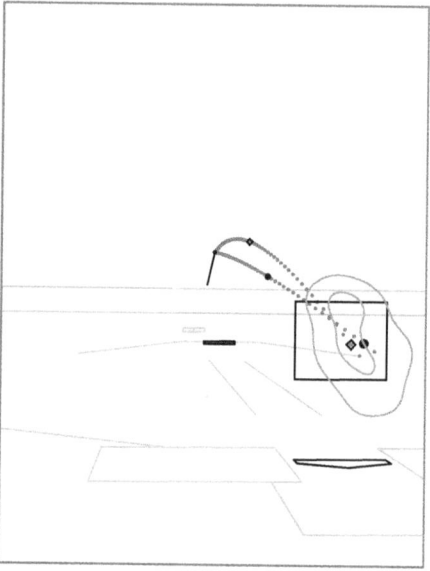

Type	Frequency	Velocity	H Movement	V Movement
● Fastball	52.1%	93 [101]	2.8 [146]	-14.3 [102]
◇ Curveball	46.5%	79.2 [102]	5.8 [93]	-58.1 [78]

Cy Sneed   RHP

Born: 10/01/92   Age: 28   Bats: R   Throws: R
Height: 6'4"   Weight: 213   Origin: Round 3, 2014 Draft (#85 overall)

YEAR	TEAM	LVL	AGE	W	L	SV	G	GS	IP	H	HR	BB/9	K/9	K	GB%	BABIP
2018	FRE	AAA	25	10	6	0	26	20	127	120	6	3.8	8.1	114	43.5%	.317
2019	RR	AAA	26	7	6	1	19	9	81^2	71	13	2.6	7.8	71	38.3%	.266
2019	HOU	MLB	26	0	1	0	8	0	21^1	26	5	2.1	9.7	23	44.6%	.356
2020	HOU	MLB	27	0	3	0	18	0	17^1	22	3	5.2	10.9	21	28.8%	.404
2021 FS	*HOU*	*MLB*	*28*	*2*	*2*	*0*	*57*	*0*	*50*	*48*	*8*	*3.4*	*8.5*	*47*	*39.3%*	*.292*

Comparables: Mike Mayers, Scott Barlow, Kyle McGowin

Sneed bears such a close resemblance to 1960s claymation prospector Yukon Cornelius that the right-hander had the nickname inscribed on his glove. The similarity ends there. Cornelius was the greatest prospector in the north, whereas Sneed struggles to get by in the south. There's no gold to be found in his numbers beyond an elevated strikeout rate, although you might find a little silver developing in his beard from a few too many baserunners and homers. The staunchest McKinseyite in the Astros org might've balked at banishing Sneed to the Island of Misfit Toys, but that didn't prevent him from joining the Yakult Swallows in early December.

YEAR	TEAM	LVL	AGE	WHIP	ERA	DRA-	WARP	MPH	FB%	WHF	CSP
2018	FRE	AAA	25	1.36	3.83	103	1.0				
2019	RR	AAA	26	1.16	4.19	59	2.9				
2019	HOU	MLB	26	1.45	5.48	107	0.0	94.6	70.3%	22.1%	
2020	HOU	MLB	27	1.85	5.71	105	0.1	95.5	69.6%	24.5%	
2021 FS	*HOU*	*MLB*	*28*	*1.34*	*4.35*	*98*	*0.3*	*95.1*	*69.9%*	*23.5%*	*49.5%*

Cy Sneed, continued

Pitch Shape vs LHH

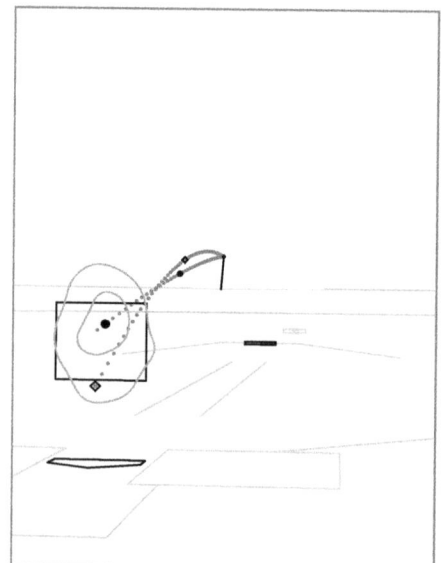

Pitch Shape vs RHH

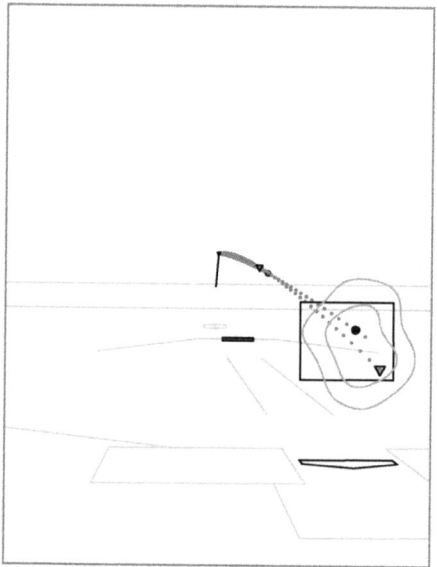

Type	Frequency	Velocity	H Movement	V Movement
● Fastball	65.8%	93.2 [102]	1.1 [138]	-12.4 [108]
▽ Slider	13.6%	82.8 [95]	9.1 [115]	-30.8 [109]
◇ Curveball	14.5%	79.9 [105]	7 [98]	-50.1 [96]

Blake Taylor LHP
Born: 08/17/95 Age: 25 Bats: L Throws: L
Height: 6'3" Weight: 220 Origin: Round 2, 2013 Draft (#51 overall)

YEAR	TEAM	LVL	AGE	W	L	SV	G	GS	IP	H	HR	BB/9	K/9	K	GB%	BABIP
2018	STL	HI-A	22	1	8	0	17	16	75²	72	4	5.4	8.6	72	49.1%	.318
2018	LV	AAA	22	2	0	0	2	2	11	11	0	7.4	9.0	11	62.1%	.393
2019	STL	HI-A	23	2	2	7	21	0	27¹	24	1	4.0	9.5	29	64.5%	.315
2019	BNG	AA	23	0	1	3	18	0	39	25	2	2.8	10.4	45	50.0%	.245
2020	HOU	MLB	24	2	1	1	22	0	20²	13	2	5.2	7.4	17	50.0%	.196
2021 FS	HOU	MLB	25	2	3	0	57	0	50	48	6	5.4	8.4	46	49.8%	.297
2021 DC	HOU	MLB	25	2	2	0	42	0	45	43	6	5.4	8.4	41	49.8%	.297

Comparables: Nestor Cortes, Randy Rosario, Dovydas Neverauskas

Like your friend who frustrates you by using the same move over and over again on *Tekken*, Taylor spammed opponents with his four-seam fastball. Hitters did no better than your attempts to defend the repetitive onslaught, proving unable to cope. Taylor's heater restricted foes to a .120 average in the regular season, with a solitary extra-base hit. It was all the more remarkable for his usage, as he threw the fifth-highest percentage of four-seamers in the league, and his whiff rate, which was unimpressive. The pitch instead draws poor contact or catches hitters looking. It cuts in an unconventional, deceptive manner, breaking away from lefties and jamming righties inside. He did mix in a slider occasionally with far less success. Major-league hitters might eventually figure out the counter that negates this strategy. For now, if it ain't broke, don't fix it.

YEAR	TEAM	LVL	AGE	WHIP	ERA	DRA-	WARP	MPH	FB%	WHF	CSP
2018	STL	HI-A	22	1.55	5.59	87	1.0				
2018	LV	AAA	22	1.82	4.09	86	0.2				
2019	STL	HI-A	23	1.32	2.63	101	-0.1				
2019	BNG	AA	23	0.95	1.85	68	0.6				
2020	HOU	MLB	24	1.21	2.18	97	0.2	95.7	76.5%	19.9%	
2021 FS	HOU	MLB	25	1.56	4.91	106	0.1	95.7	76.5%	19.9%	50.6%
2021 DC	HOU	MLB	25	1.56	4.91	106	0.1	95.7	76.5%	19.9%	50.6%

Blake Taylor, continued

Pitch Shape vs LHH

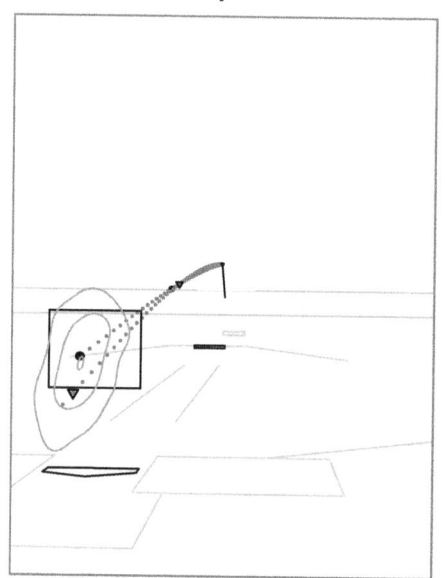

Pitch Shape vs RHH

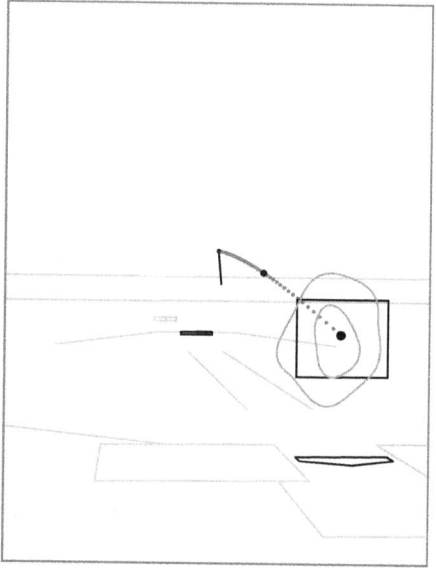

Type	Frequency	Velocity	H Movement	V Movement
● Fastball	75.7%	93.8 [104]	-1.2 [138]	-13.5 [105]
▽ Slider	22.3%	85.1 [105]	-5.9 [102]	-32.9 [102]

Jose Urquidy   RHP

Born: 05/01/95   Age: 26   Bats: R   Throws: R
Height: 6'0"   Weight: 217   Origin: International Free Agent, 2015

YEAR	TEAM	LVL	AGE	W	L	SV	G	GS	IP	H	HR	BB/9	K/9	K	GB%	BABIP
2018	TRI	SS	23	0	0	0	4	4	11^1	15	0	1.6	7.9	10	39.5%	.395
2018	FAY	HI-A	23	2	2	0	9	7	46	40	2	1.6	7.4	38	48.9%	.284
2019	CC	AA	24	2	2	0	7	6	33	28	2	1.4	10.9	40	42.0%	.302
2019	RR	AAA	24	5	3	0	13	12	70	67	15	2.1	12.1	94	31.9%	.313
2019	HOU	MLB	24	2	1	0	9	7	41	38	6	1.5	8.8	40	35.0%	.286
2020	HOU	MLB	25	1	1	0	5	5	29^2	22	4	2.4	5.2	17	35.6%	.209
2021 FS	HOU	MLB	26	9	8	0	26	26	150	145	28	2.6	8.2	136	36.1%	.286
2021 DC	HOU	MLB	26	9	8	0	25	25	147.7	143	27	2.6	8.2	134	36.1%	.286

Comparables: Kevin Gausman, Luke Weaver, Rafael Montero

If all you knew about Urquidy's season was his ERA, his WHIP and that he was back on the mound for three playoff starts, plus an appearance in a decisive Game 7 of the ALCS, you might assume that he'd spent six months successfully building upon the stellar World Series start he delivered for Houston a year prior. All you would have missed from the narrative was a scandal that rocked baseball, a global pandemic and Urquidy's own positive COVID-19 test that limited him to a handful of regular season turns. The stuff didn't play nearly as well when it came to missing bats, and as a result the underlying numbers were much less encouraging than those from his debut. The Astros were either unconcerned by such a small sample or decided their decimated staff was not in a position to do without Urquidy in the postseason rotation. For everyone's sake, let's hope that 2021 is less turbulent.

YEAR	TEAM	LVL	AGE	WHIP	ERA	DRA-	WARP	MPH	FB%	WHF	CSP
2018	TRI	SS	23	1.50	2.38	297	-1.1				
2018	FAY	HI-A	23	1.04	2.35	78	0.9				
2019	CC	AA	24	1.00	4.09	63	0.7				
2019	RR	AAA	24	1.19	4.63	59	2.6				
2019	HOU	MLB	24	1.10	3.95	88	0.6	95.3	47.3%	28.3%	
2020	HOU	MLB	25	1.01	2.73	138	-0.3	94.9	54.5%	20.9%	
2021 FS	HOU	MLB	26	1.27	4.13	94	2.0	95.1	50.8%	24.7%	50.9%
2021 DC	HOU	MLB	26	1.27	4.13	94	1.9	95.1	50.8%	24.7%	50.9%

Jose Urquidy, continued

Pitch Shape vs LHH

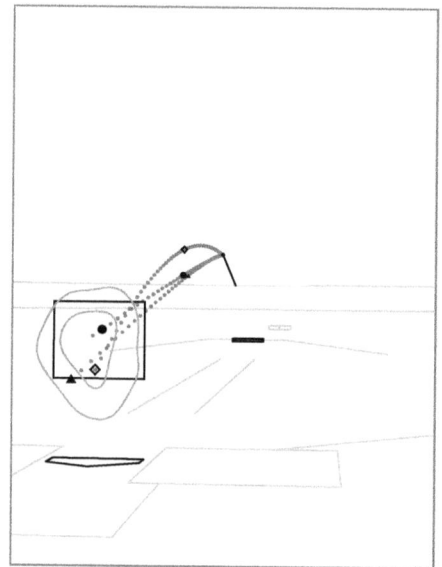

Pitch Shape vs RHH

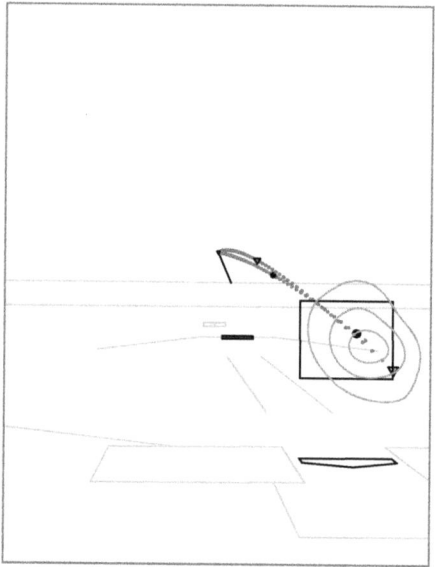

Type	Frequency	Velocity	H Movement	V Movement
● Fastball	54.5%	93.3 [102]	-6.7 [100]	-11 [112]
▲ Changeup	20.5%	84.5 [97]	-15 [82]	-25.7 [105]
▽ Slider	13.1%	79.4 [80]	14.1 [133]	-37.6 [89]
◇ Curveball	11.9%	77 [94]	9.6 [108]	-55.4 [84]

Framber Valdez LHP

Born: 11/19/93 Age: 27 Bats: L Throws: L
Height: 5'11" Weight: 239 Origin: International Free Agent, 2015

YEAR	TEAM	LVL	AGE	W	L	SV	G	GS	IP	H	HR	BB/9	K/9	K	GB%	BABIP
2018	CC	AA	24	4	5	1	20	13	94^1	92	7	2.8	11.4	120	56.8%	.365
2018	FRE	AAA	24	2	0	0	2	1	8^2	8	0	3.1	9.3	9	47.8%	.348
2018	HOU	MLB	24	4	1	0	8	5	37	22	3	5.8	8.3	34	69.6%	.213
2019	RR	AAA	25	5	2	1	10	7	44^1	29	3	3.5	13.8	68	72.2%	.302
2019	HOU	MLB	25	4	7	0	26	8	70^2	74	9	5.6	8.7	68	62.0%	.319
2020	HOU	MLB	26	5	3	0	11	10	70^2	63	5	2.0	9.7	76	59.7%	.314
2021 FS	HOU	MLB	27	10	7	0	26	26	150	133	15	4.3	10.4	173	59.4%	.311
2021 DC	HOU	MLB	27	10	8	0	27	27	159.7	142	16	4.3	10.4	184	59.4%	.311

Comparables: Max Fried, Ryan Borucki, Matt Hall

Two identical samples in back-to-back seasons. The first cast doubts over Valdez's chances to stick in the majors; the second left observers wondering how Houston could possibly have done without him. What changed? Given the year, the team and the repertoire, the obvious answer is that Valdez turned to his elite curveball far more often. What actually happened was as much of a mindset adjustment as a technical change, as the southpaw worked with the team's mental skills coaches to find the focus and composure that so often eluded him in blow-ups throughout 2019. There was a pitch mix tweak too, as the four-seam was largely shelved in favor of more sinkers, and the composure extended to his control, with his walk rate more than halved. The curve was utilized at the same rate and remained exceptional, providing the majority of Valdez's strikeouts and helping him finish with the third-best DRA among AL starters. By the end of the playoffs, the team appeared to trust him more than any other starter. A much larger sample should be forthcoming.

YEAR	TEAM	LVL	AGE	WHIP	ERA	DRA-	WARP	MPH	FB%	WHF	CSP
2018	CC	AA	24	1.28	4.10	72	1.8				
2018	FRE	AAA	24	1.27	4.15	100	0.1				
2018	HOU	MLB	24	1.24	2.19	136	-0.4	94.4	69.0%	22.9%	
2019	RR	AAA	25	1.04	3.25	27	2.3				
2019	HOU	MLB	25	1.67	5.86	116	-0.1	95.5	61.4%	26.1%	
2020	HOU	MLB	26	1.12	3.57	68	1.8	95.4	58.6%	24.4%	
2021 FS	HOU	MLB	27	1.37	3.85	87	2.5	95.3	60.8%	24.9%	49.4%
2021 DC	HOU	MLB	27	1.37	3.85	87	2.5	95.3	60.8%	24.9%	49.4%

Houston Astros 2021

Framber Valdez, continued

Pitch Shape vs LHH

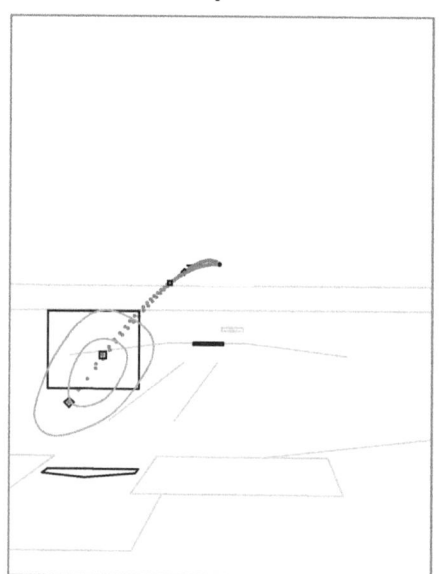

Pitch Shape vs RHH

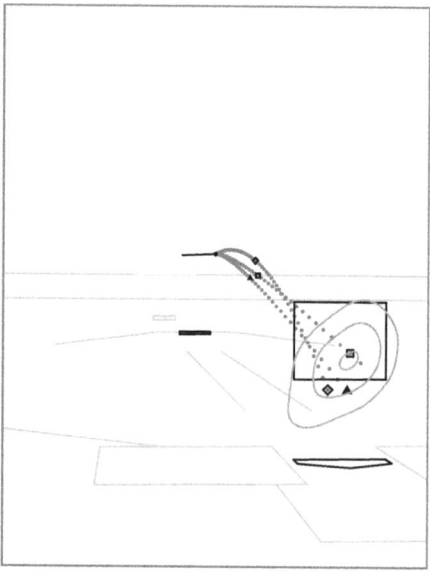

Type	Frequency	Velocity	H Movement	V Movement
● Fastball	3.1%	93.9 [104]	3.3 [116]	-17.3 [94]
□ Sinker	55.5%	93.1 [103]	11.4 [112]	-23.4 [91]
▲ Changeup	7.9%	88.7 [114]	11.6 [100]	-29.6 [94]
◇ Curveball	33.5%	80.7 [108]	-11.9 [118]	-50.5 [95]

PLAYER COMMENTS WITHOUT GRAPHS

Yordan Alvarez OF
Born: 06/27/97 Age: 24 Bats: L Throws: R
Height: 6'5" Weight: 225 Origin: International Free Agent, 2016

YEAR	TEAM	LVL	AGE	PA	R	2B	3B	HR	RBI	BB	K	SB	CS	AVG/OBP/SLG
2018	CC	AA	21	190	39	13	0	12	46	19	45	5	2	.325/.389/.615
2018	FRE	AAA	21	189	24	8	0	8	28	23	47	1	0	.259/.349/.452
2019	RR	AAA	22	253	50	16	0	23	71	38	50	2	1	.343/.443/.742
2019	HOU	MLB	22	369	58	26	0	27	78	52	94	0	0	.313/.412/.655
2020	HOU	MLB	23	9	2	0	0	1	4	0	1	0	0	.250/.333/.625
2021 FS	HOU	MLB	24	600	101	29	1	37	106	71	162	1	1	.271/.366/.547
2021 DC	HOU	MLB	24	523	88	25	1	33	93	62	141	1	1	.271/.366/.547

Comparables: Mark McGwire, Fred McGriff, Giancarlo Stanton

In hindsight, Alvarez's knee trouble was the early warning that the 2020 Astros would not live up to the lofty standards they set over the past three seasons. The 2019 Rookie of the Year's absence robbed them of one of their most potent weapons. His recovery wasn't helped by a COVID-19 diagnosis but that may have just delayed the inevitable surgery he underwent on both knees. This declining offense desperately needs him back at full strength in 2021 if they're to have any hope of becoming feared once again.

YEAR	TEAM	LVL	AGE	PA	DRC+	BABIP	BRR	FRAA	WARP
2018	CC	AA	21	190	164	.377	0.2	LF(31): 3.6, 1B(5): -0.1	1.6
2018	FRE	AAA	21	189	109	.315	-2.0	LF(34): -6.3	-0.5
2019	RR	AAA	22	253	176	.355	-2.3	LF(27): 0.3, 1B(9): -1.1, RF(2): -0.2	2.4
2019	HOU	MLB	22	369	148	.366	-0.5	LF(10): -0.5	2.8
2020	HOU	MLB	23	9	88	.167	-0.2		0.0
2021 FS	HOU	MLB	24	600	138	.329	-0.8	1B 0, LF 0	4.3
2021 DC	HOU	MLB	24	523	138	.329	-0.7		3.4

Ronnie Dawson OF

Born: 05/19/95 Age: 26 Bats: L Throws: R
Height: 6'2" Weight: 217 Origin: Round 2, 2016 Draft (#61 overall)

YEAR	TEAM	LVL	AGE	PA	R	2B	3B	HR	RBI	BB	K	SB	CS	AVG/OBP/SLG
2018	FAY	HI-A	23	376	51	18	1	10	49	39	96	29	11	.247/.331/.398
2018	CC	AA	23	123	18	6	1	6	14	6	34	6	3	.289/.341/.518
2019	CC	AA	24	459	71	20	2	17	50	47	141	13	10	.212/.320/.403
2019	RR	AAA	24	39	1	1	0	0	3	3	11	1	0	.147/.231/.176
2021 FS	*HOU*	*MLB*	*26*	*600*	*73*	*24*	*2*	*18*	*69*	*45*	*198*	*12*	*7*	*.207/.281/.361*
2021 DC	*HOU*	*MLB*	*26*	*173*	*21*	*7*	*0*	*5*	*19*	*13*	*57*	*3*	*2*	*.207/.281/.361*

Comparables: Joe Benson, Matthew den Dekker, Tommy Pham

As Houston dealt with an outfield exodus, the athletic Dawson was one of the few obvious upper-minors names available for depth. In that light, their decision to not add him to the 40-man ahead of the Rule 5 draft—for the second consecutive year—offers little encouragement for his chances of finding even a part-time role.

YEAR	TEAM	LVL	AGE	PA	DRC+	BABIP	BRR	FRAA	WARP
2018	FAY	HI-A	23	376	116	.317	-2.3	CF(88): 4.8	1.3
2018	CC	AA	23	123	113	.365	1.9	CF(24): 0.1, RF(5): -0.4	0.4
2019	CC	AA	24	459	97	.281	1.1	CF(78): -2.6, RF(10): -0.7, LF(2): 2.6	1.3
2019	RR	AAA	24	39	25	.208	0.1	CF(6): -0.5, RF(4): -0.0	-0.2
2021 FS	*HOU*	*MLB*	*26*	*600*	*71*	*.291*	*0.9*	*CF 4, LF 5*	*0.7*
2021 DC	*HOU*	*MLB*	*26*	*173*	*71*	*.291*	*0.3*	*CF 1, LF 2*	*0.2*

Taylor Jones 1B

Born: 12/06/93 Age: 27 Bats: R Throws: R
Height: 6'7" Weight: 230 Origin: Round 19, 2016 Draft (#577 overall)

YEAR	TEAM	LVL	AGE	PA	R	2B	3B	HR	RBI	BB	K	SB	CS	AVG/OBP/SLG
2018	CC	AA	24	367	45	25	1	13	63	45	78	2	0	.314/.409/.528
2018	FRE	AAA	24	163	16	7	1	5	17	16	46	0	0	.210/.294/.378
2019	RR	AAA	25	531	86	28	0	22	84	68	112	0	1	.291/.388/.501
2020	HOU	MLB	26	22	3	1	0	1	3	1	7	0	0	.190/.227/.381
2021 FS	HOU	MLB	27	600	81	24	1	23	76	57	184	0	0	.224/.313/.408
2021 DC	HOU	MLB	27	126	17	5	0	5	16	12	38	0	0	.224/.313/.408

Comparables: Chris Duncan, Matt Olson, Matt Clark

Jones has been late to a lot of things. He transitioned to hitting late, spending his initial college years predominantly on the mound. He started trying out positions other than first base even later, playing both third and left field for the first time in 2019. He was late to debut in the majors, doing so at the age of 26 after this complicated path through pro ball. It's impressive that he made it at all, in a lot of ways, but merely turning up at some point isn't going to cut it now. Jones needs to be on time at the plate, or he'll never get enough of his raw pop into games to be anything but an occasional party-crasher.

YEAR	TEAM	LVL	AGE	PA	DRC+	BABIP	BRR	FRAA	WARP
2018	CC	AA	24	367	160	.377	-3.2	1B(70): 4.1, LF(7): -0.8	1.9
2018	FRE	AAA	24	163	82	.266	-1.3	1B(29): -1.6, LF(1): -0.3	-0.6
2019	RR	AAA	25	531	122	.336	-1.7	1B(68): 6.3, LF(27): 0.5, 3B(15): 1.0	2.9
2020	HOU	MLB	26	22	86	.231	-0.3	1B(3): -0.4	-0.1
2021 FS	HOU	MLB	27	600	92	.299	-1.0	LF 0, RF -4	-0.1
2021 DC	HOU	MLB	27	126	92	.299	-0.2	LF 0, RF -1	0.0

Houston Astros 2021

Chas McCormick RF
Born: 04/19/95 Age: 26 Bats: R Throws: L
Height: 6'0" Weight: 208 Origin: Round 21, 2017 Draft (#631 overall)

YEAR	TEAM	LVL	AGE	PA	R	2B	3B	HR	RBI	BB	K	SB	CS	AVG/OBP/SLG
2018	FAY	HI-A	23	209	26	13	3	2	27	19	34	7	0	.264/.332/.401
2018	CC	AA	23	282	33	10	1	2	28	24	32	12	4	.280/.344/.352
2019	CC	AA	24	223	26	3	3	4	22	39	28	9	3	.277/.426/.395
2019	RR	AAA	24	225	39	3	3	10	44	28	34	7	1	.262/.347/.466
2021 FS	HOU	MLB	26	600	78	24	3	14	67	54	119	6	2	.248/.325/.388
2021 DC	HOU	MLB	26	243	31	9	1	5	27	21	48	2	1	.248/.325/.388

Comparables: Jerry Owens, Mike Tauchman, JB Shuck

While several organizations named high-end prospects with no major-league experience to their postseason rosters, Houston's addition of McCormick prompted one prevailing response: "Who?" Lack of respect for the Pennsylvania State Athletic Conference aside, McCormick has excellent minor-league plate discipline numbers with burgeoning power, but there's doubt it'll play in the bigs, a concern the Astros are poised to test.

YEAR	TEAM	LVL	AGE	PA	DRC+	BABIP	BRR	FRAA	WARP
2018	FAY	HI-A	23	209	109	.305	0.9	RF(44): 1.9, LF(7): 0.0	0.5
2018	CC	AA	23	282	108	.308	-0.2	RF(24): 1.9, LF(23): -1.8, CF(22): 1.0	0.4
2019	CC	AA	24	223	151	.310	0.7	LF(40): 5.2, CF(6): -0.3, RF(3): -0.9	2.1
2019	RR	AAA	24	225	101	.261	0.0	RF(22): 0.2, CF(16): 0.6, LF(12): 1.2	0.8
2021 FS	HOU	MLB	26	600	94	.296	0.1	RF 4, LF 1	1.6
2021 DC	HOU	MLB	26	243	94	.296	0.0	RF 2, LF 0	0.5

Freudis Nova SS
Born: 01/12/00 Age: 21 Bats: R Throws: R
Height: 6'1" Weight: 180 Origin: International Free Agent, 2016

YEAR	TEAM	LVL	AGE	PA	R	2B	3B	HR	RBI	BB	K	SB	CS	AVG/OBP/SLG
2018	AST	ROK	18	157	21	3	1	6	28	6	21	9	5	.308/.331/.466
2019	QC	LO-A	19	299	35	20	1	3	29	15	67	10	7	.259/.301/.369
2021 FS	HOU	MLB	21	600	46	23	2	9	51	29	172	11	7	.211/.254/.309

Comparables: Tim Beckham, Ryan Mountcastle, Javy Guerra

When it comes to prospects, it's not nature or nurture so much as nature and nurture. Nova's standing to date has largely been driven by the former, thanks to his projectable frame, defensive athleticism and bat speed. Missing a full season of pro ball-related activities will offer some insight into how much of the latter he needs to become a big-league regular.

YEAR	TEAM	LVL	AGE	PA	DRC+	BABIP	BRR	FRAA	WARP
2018	AST	ROK	18	157		.317			
2019	QC	LO-A	19	299	104	.330	-0.4	SS(32): -3.0, 2B(23): -0.0, 3B(18): -0.6	0.8
2021 FS	HOU	MLB	21	600	52	.287	1.0	SS -6, 2B 0	-2.6

Jeremy Peña SS
Born: 09/22/97 Age: 23 Bats: R Throws: R
Height: 6'0" Weight: 202 Origin: Round 3, 2018 Draft (#102 overall)

YEAR	TEAM	LVL	AGE	PA	R	2B	3B	HR	RBI	BB	K	SB	CS	AVG/OBP/SLG
2018	TRI	SS	20	156	22	5	0	1	10	18	19	3	0	.250/.340/.309
2019	QC	LO-A	21	289	44	8	4	5	41	35	57	17	6	.293/.389/.421
2019	FAY	HI-A	21	185	28	13	3	2	13	12	33	3	4	.317/.378/.467
2021 FS	HOU	MLB	23	600	73	24	3	11	63	42	150	7	5	.239/.302/.360
2021 DC	HOU	MLB	23	69	8	2	0	1	7	4	17	0	1	.239/.302/.360

Comparables: Darnell Sweeney, Zach Walters, Andy Burns

The Astros were so focused on stocking their 60-man roster with players who would help in 2020 that for much of the season, they had none of their top prospects at Corpus Christi. Peña was one of the few who joined the group in September, speaking to Houston's high opinion of the middle infielder. Given his broad range of skills, there's already a strong base for a major-league contributor of some sort. The team expects greater things, with the belief there's more power in the bat than he's shown to date. It's an exciting thought for a player who was already riding significant buzz from 2019: a version of Peña with home run pop would be one of the most well-rounded prospects in the game.

YEAR	TEAM	LVL	AGE	PA	DRC+	BABIP	BRR	FRAA	WARP
2018	TRI	SS	20	156	133	.282	-1.0	SS(32): -0.5, 2B(4): 0.0	0.5
2019	QC	LO-A	21	289	153	.357	3.3	SS(60): -2.1, 2B(2): -0.3	2.9
2019	FAY	HI-A	21	185	144	.383	1.8	SS(29): -0.2, 2B(11): 0.1, 3B(1): -0.0	1.7
2021 FS	HOU	MLB	23	600	82	.310	0.4	SS -5, 2B 0	0.0
2021 DC	HOU	MLB	23	69	82	.310	0.0	SS -1	0.0

Steven Souza Jr. RF

Born: 04/24/89   Age: 32   Bats: R   Throws: R
Height: 6'4"   Weight: 225   Origin: Round 3, 2007 Draft (#100 overall)

YEAR	TEAM	LVL	AGE	PA	R	2B	3B	HR	RBI	BB	K	SB	CS	AVG/OBP/SLG
2018	ARI	MLB	29	272	21	15	3	5	29	28	75	6	1	.220/.309/.369
2020	CHC	MLB	31	31	3	2	0	1	5	4	15	1	0	.148/.258/.333
2021 FS	HOU	MLB	32	600	66	22	2	21	71	67	219	12	5	.210/.309/.388

Comparables: Rob Deer, Dustan Mohr, Jayson Werth

That Souza was able to play at all in 2020 qualifies as a victory, as he missed the preceding season after tearing the ACL, LCL, PCL and posterior lateral capsule in his left knee during spring training. That he was essentially the only major-league addition the Cubs made heading into the year was an indictment on the Ricketts' cheapness. That he was released after just 31 plate appearances—during which he whiffed on nearly half his swings—makes it fair to wonder if he has anything left to offer a major-league team.

YEAR	TEAM	LVL	AGE	PA	DRC+	BABIP	BRR	FRAA	WARP
2018	ARI	MLB	29	272	77	.298	0.1	RF(65): -5.9, CF(1): -0.0	-0.8
2020	CHC	MLB	31	31	65	.273	0.0	RF(6): -0.3, LF(3): 0.0	-0.1
2021 FS	HOU	MLB	32	600	90	.313	0.8	RF -2, LF 0	0.4

Myles Straw CF

Born: 10/17/94   Age: 26   Bats: R   Throws: R
Height: 5'10"   Weight: 178   Origin: Round 12, 2015 Draft (#349 overall)

YEAR	TEAM	LVL	AGE	PA	R	2B	3B	HR	RBI	BB	K	SB	CS	AVG/OBP/SLG
2018	CC	AA	23	294	47	7	3	1	17	35	42	35	6	.327/.414/.390
2018	FRE	AAA	23	304	48	10	3	0	14	38	60	35	3	.257/.349/.317
2018	HOU	MLB	23	10	4	0	0	1	1	1	0	2	0	.333/.400/.667
2019	RR	AAA	24	313	46	11	3	1	33	32	50	19	4	.321/.391/.394
2019	HOU	MLB	24	128	27	4	2	0	7	19	24	8	1	.269/.378/.343
2020	HOU	MLB	25	86	8	4	0	0	8	4	22	6	2	.207/.244/.256
2021 FS	HOU	MLB	26	600	77	24	3	7	57	57	147	21	7	.254/.329/.353
2021 DC	HOU	MLB	26	434	56	17	2	5	41	41	106	15	5	.254/.329/.353

Comparables: Tony Scott, Aaron Hicks, Jim Nettles

Straw hit the ball in the air more often in 2020. For a man who has more pro seasons under his belt than home runs, that's the equivalent of taking a Formula One car off-road. As if that wasn't enough of a penalty to his offensive performance, he stalled in the box with alarming regularity, striking out in more than a quarter of plate appearances. He did get to spend more time in the outfield, where his wheels can be put to better use. As far as Straw's chances of being more than a backup go, the plate is where the rubber meets the road. The majors are probably just a class above where he should be competing in that regard.

YEAR	TEAM	LVL	AGE	PA	DRC+	BABIP	BRR	FRAA	WARP
2018	CC	AA	23	294	141	.386	4.4	CF(58): 6.0, RF(6): 2.0	2.8
2018	FRE	AAA	23	304	94	.330	3.8	CF(43): 4.9, RF(25): 1.4, SS(1): -0.0	1.4
2018	HOU	MLB	23	10	108	.250	0.7	RF(5): -0.1, CF(3): -0.0, LF(1): 0.1	0.1
2019	RR	AAA	24	313	105	.386	2.5	CF(31): 4.9, SS(30): -1.1, 2B(5): -0.4	1.9
2019	HOU	MLB	24	128	91	.345	3.5	SS(26): 1.4, CF(11): -0.8, LF(8): 0.3	0.8
2020	HOU	MLB	25	86	78	.283	-0.3	CF(27): -1.6, SS(1): -0.0	-0.3
2021 FS	HOU	MLB	26	600	90	.338	1.5	CF 10, 2B 0	2.2
2021 DC	HOU	MLB	26	434	90	.338	1.1	CF 7	1.7

Garrett Stubbs   C

Born: 05/26/93   Age: 28   Bats: L   Throws: R
Height: 5'10"   Weight: 170   Origin: Round 8, 2015 Draft (#229 overall)

YEAR	TEAM	LVL	AGE	PA	R	2B	3B	HR	RBI	BB	K	SB	CS	AVG/OBP/SLG
2018	FRE	AAA	25	340	60	19	6	4	38	35	53	6	0	.310/.382/.455
2019	RR	AAA	26	235	33	11	0	7	23	24	38	12	2	.240/.332/.397
2019	HOU	MLB	26	39	8	3	0	0	2	4	7	1	0	.200/.282/.286
2020	HOU	MLB	27	10	1	0	0	0	1	0	0	0	1	.125/.111/.125
2021 FS	HOU	MLB	28	600	74	23	2	15	67	57	112	4	2	.234/.318/.374
2021 DC	HOU	MLB	28	63	7	2	0	1	7	6	11	0	0	.234/.318/.374

Comparables: Raffy Lopez, Carlos Ruiz, Vinny Rottino

While we argue about the three-true-outcomes problem in modern baseball, Stubbs was busy doing something about it: all of his plate appearances ended in a ball in play. It might turn out to be more of an argument in TTO's favor, but let's see him do it over a few hundred plate appearances before we rush to judgement.

YEAR	TEAM	P. COUNT	FRM RUNS	BLK RUNS	THRW RUNS	TOT RUNS
2018	FRE	11107	7.8	0.2	1.5	9.1
2019	HOU	1145	-0.5	-0.9	0.0	-1.4
2020	HOU	400	0.1	0.0	0.0	0.1
2021	HOU	2405	0.0	-0.5	0.0	-0.5
2021	HOU	2405	0.0	-0.5	0.0	-0.5

YEAR	TEAM	LVL	AGE	PA	DRC+	BABIP	BRR	FRAA	WARP
2018	FRE	AAA	25	340	117	.361	3.0	C(75): 10.5, RF(2): -0.2, 1B(1): -0.0	3.2
2019	RR	AAA	26	235	85	.261	0.7	C(54): 8.8, 2B(5): -0.8, LF(1): -0.1	1.5
2019	HOU	MLB	26	39	79	.250	0.2	C(11): -1.5, LF(7): -0.1, RF(1): -0.0	-0.1
2020	HOU	MLB	27	10	93	.111	-0.1	C(8): -0.0, LF(3): 0.1	0.0
2021 FS	HOU	MLB	28	600	88	.271	-0.3	C -3, 1B 0	1.2
2021 DC	HOU	MLB	28	63	88	.271	0.0	C 0	0.1

Bryan Abreu   RHP

Born: 04/22/97   Age: 24   Bats: R   Throws: R
Height: 6'1"   Weight: 225   Origin: International Free Agent, 2013

YEAR	TEAM	LVL	AGE	W	L	SV	G	GS	IP	H	HR	BB/9	K/9	K	GB%	BABIP
2018	TRI	SS	21	2	0	0	4	2	16	11	2	3.4	12.4	22	29.4%	.281
2018	QC	LO-A	21	4	1	3	10	5	38^1	22	2	4.0	16.0	68	47.0%	.317
2019	FAY	HI-A	22	1	0	0	3	3	14^2	9	2	3.7	15.3	25	38.5%	.292
2019	CC	AA	22	6	2	2	20	13	76^2	60	6	5.6	11.9	101	42.5%	.310
2019	HOU	MLB	22	0	0	0	7	0	8^2	4	0	3.1	13.5	13	50.0%	.250
2020	HOU	MLB	23	0	0	0	4	0	3^1	1	0	18.9	8.1	3	37.5%	.125
2021 FS	HOU	MLB	24	2	3	0	57	0	50	44	8	5.8	10.8	59	40.7%	.297
2021 DC	HOU	MLB	24	0	0	0	10	0	28	24	4	5.8	10.8	33	40.7%	.297

Comparables: Jorge Alcala, Cristian Javier, Demarcus Evans

Dreams of an elite bullpen piece remain just that as far as Abreu is concerned. With a lively fastball and slider/curve combo and with potential yet to be realized, the hope was that Abreu could harness some command to become a late-inning weapon. Instead he showed up lacking not only the command but also the velocity. The 95-plus heat evaporated, as his brief follow-up saw him struggle to average 93 with little idea of where anything was going. The Astros cited poor conditioning and overthinking as the causes of Abreu's struggles, demoting him after he walked seven of the 20 batters he faced.

YEAR	TEAM	LVL	AGE	WHIP	ERA	DRA-	WARP	MPH	FB%	WHF	CSP
2018	TRI	SS	21	1.06	1.12	273	-1.4				
2018	QC	LO-A	21	1.02	1.64	55	1.1				
2019	FAY	HI-A	22	1.02	3.68	63	0.3				
2019	CC	AA	22	1.41	5.05	87	0.6				
2019	HOU	MLB	22	0.81	1.04	95	0.1	96.6	32.2%	46.8%	
2020	HOU	MLB	23	2.40	2.70	121	0.0	94.8	35.5%	23.5%	
2021 FS	HOU	MLB	24	1.53	5.01	106	0.1	95.8	33.7%	36.6%	39.8%
2021 DC	HOU	MLB	24	1.53	5.01	106	0.0	95.8	33.7%	36.6%	39.8%

Roberto Osuna   RHP
Born: 02/07/95   Age: 26   Bats: R   Throws: R
Height: 6'2"   Weight: 217   Origin: International Free Agent, 2011

YEAR	TEAM	LVL	AGE	W	L	SV	G	GS	IP	H	HR	BB/9	K/9	K	GB%	BABIP
2018	HOU	MLB	23	2	2	12	23	0	22^2	17	1	1.2	7.5	19	44.4%	.258
2018	TOR	MLB	23	0	0	9	15	0	15^1	16	0	0.6	7.6	13	38.3%	.340
2019	HOU	MLB	24	4	3	38	66	0	65	45	8	1.7	10.1	73	39.2%	.236
2020	HOU	MLB	25	0	0	1	4	0	4^1	3	0	0.0	6.2	3	61.5%	.231
2021 FS	HOU	MLB	26	3	2	0	57	0	50	42	7	2.2	9.6	53	40.2%	.281

Comparables: Huston Street, Keone Kela, Yimi García

A year after Brandon Taubman's Osuna-defending outburst that led to the assistant GM's termination, Houston removed Osuna himself from the organization rather more quietly. The decision seemed obvious when elbow trouble ended his season after four appearances and the initial recommendation was Tommy John surgery. It was slightly less obvious when a second opinion suggested Osuna could rehab the injury without surgery, with the closer playing catch before the season was over. The kicker was the $10 million or so that he was likely to earn in arbitration, leading the Astros to put him on waivers at the first available opportunity. That it took money and health to bring about the end of Osuna's tenure in Houston should surprise no one. In reality, the obvious decision was the one they should have taken two and a half years earlier, when considering whether to trade for a player who was arrested and suspended for domestic abuse.

Houston Astros 2021

YEAR	TEAM	LVL	AGE	WHIP	ERA	DRA-	WARP	MPH	FB%	WHF	CSP
2018	HOU	MLB	23	0.88	1.99	79	0.4	96.8	47.4%	29.1%	
2018	TOR	MLB	23	1.11	2.93	88	0.2	97.5	67.4%	23.8%	
2019	HOU	MLB	24	0.88	2.63	72	1.3	98.6	49.3%	34.2%	
2020	HOU	MLB	25	0.69	2.08	89	0.1	96.0	46.3%	28.6%	
2021 FS	HOU	MLB	26	1.10	3.04	73	1.0	98.1	50.4%	32.3%	47.5%

Brad Peacock RHP

Born: 02/02/88   Age: 33   Bats: R   Throws: R
Height: 6'1"   Weight: 207   Origin: Round 41, 2006 Draft (#1231 overall)

YEAR	TEAM	LVL	AGE	W	L	SV	G	GS	IP	H	HR	BB/9	K/9	K	GB%	BABIP
2018	HOU	MLB	30	3	5	3	61	1	65	56	11	2.8	13.3	96	37.3%	.317
2019	HOU	MLB	31	7	6	0	23	15	91^2	78	15	3.0	9.4	96	37.8%	.267
2020	HOU	MLB	32	0	0	0	3	0	2^1	3	0	3.9	11.6	3	28.6%	.429
2021 FS	HOU	MLB	33	2	2	0	57	0	50	45	9	3.4	9.8	54	38.2%	.289

Comparables: Trevor Cahill, Jhoulys Chacín, Joe Kelly

Millions tuned in to Peacock in 2020—the streaming service, that is. The days of appointment viewing for the Astros righty appear to be long gone. Two full ticks came off the fastball, with none of the swing-and-miss stuff that generated his peak ratings. A nerve issue in his neck was followed by shoulder discomfort, and it was the shoulder that got him taken off the air after three episodes. He's unlikely to be renewed for another season in Houston. Finally a free agent at the age of 33, Peacock's timing couldn't be worse for entering the market. Comcast's turned out to be excellent, though.

YEAR	TEAM	LVL	AGE	WHIP	ERA	DRA-	WARP	MPH	FB%	WHF	CSP
2018	HOU	MLB	30	1.17	3.46	56	1.8	94.6	54.6%	31.6%	
2019	HOU	MLB	31	1.19	4.12	104	0.6	93.8	58.5%	21.7%	
2020	HOU	MLB	32	1.71	7.71	91	0.0	91.8	50.8%	22.7%	
2021 FS	HOU	MLB	33	1.29	4.16	93	0.4	94.0	57.2%	24.4%	46.7%

Austin Pruitt RHP

Born: 08/31/89   Age: 31   Bats: R   Throws: R
Height: 5'10"   Weight: 185   Origin: Round 9, 2013 Draft (#278 overall)

YEAR	TEAM	LVL	AGE	W	L	SV	G	GS	IP	H	HR	BB/9	K/9	K	GB%	BABIP
2018	DUR	AAA	28	3	0	1	14	4	39^2	26	2	1.6	11.1	49	48.9%	.261
2018	TB	MLB	28	2	3	4	23	0	69^2	72	7	2.1	5.4	42	49.1%	.290
2019	DUR	AAA	29	3	3	0	18	6	48^1	61	9	2.2	9.5	51	48.7%	.364
2019	TB	MLB	29	3	0	0	14	2	47	47	7	2.3	7.5	39	52.1%	.301
2021 FS	HOU	MLB	31	2	2	0	57	0	50	48	7	2.1	8.0	44	47.6%	.291
2021 DC	HOU	MLB	31	2	2	0	53	0	39.3	38	5	2.1	8.0	34	47.6%	.291

Comparables: Erasmo Ramírez, Joe Biagini, Chris Stratton

A hairline fracture that cost Pruitt the entire season came as something of a surprise, as the former Ray appeared confident in July that his elbow discomfort was not that serious. His acquisition was the last move made by Jeff Luhnow, who apparently felt the same way about his players making a racket in the dugout.

YEAR	TEAM	LVL	AGE	WHIP	ERA	DRA-	WARP	MPH	FB%	WHF	CSP
2018	DUR	AAA	28	0.83	2.95	41	1.5				
2018	TB	MLB	28	1.26	4.65	81	1.0	93.2	43.9%	20.3%	
2019	DUR	AAA	29	1.51	5.40	104	0.6				
2019	TB	MLB	29	1.26	4.40	97	0.3	93.2	44.0%	24.9%	
2021 FS	HOU	MLB	31	1.20	3.57	85	0.7	93.2	44.0%	23.0%	48.4%
2021 DC	HOU	MLB	31	1.20	3.57	85	0.5	93.2	44.0%	23.0%	48.4%

Alex Santos II RHP
Born: 02/10/02   Age: 19   Bats: R   Throws: R
Height: 6'3"   Weight: 185   Origin: Round 2, 2020 Draft (#72 overall)

Stripped of their first- and second-round picks as a punishment for the sign-stealing scandal, Houston would have been without a top-100 choice entirely were it not for the compensation pick at 72nd overall from Gerrit Cole signing with New York. There was some symmetry to the selection, although Santos himself may not be delighted: he's a lifelong Yankees fan from the Bronx. He possesses an impressively deep arsenal for a high-school pitcher with a fastball already sitting in the mid-90s. Perhaps most important given the team that drafted him, he spent much of the pre-draft period at his father's baseball academy with a Rapsodo machine tracking his sessions for scouts. Santos might have preferred to join Cole in New York, but he may have landed in the best place to maximize his development as a pitcher.

Houston Astros 2021

Joe Smith   RHP
Born: 03/22/84   Age: 37   Bats: R   Throws: R
Height: 6'2"   Weight: 211   Origin: Round 3, 2006 Draft (#94 overall)

YEAR	TEAM	LVL	AGE	W	L	SV	G	GS	IP	H	HR	BB/9	K/9	K	GB%	BABIP
2018	HOU	MLB	34	5	1	0	56	0	45^2	34	7	2.4	9.1	46	43.3%	.239
2019	HOU	MLB	35	1	0	0	28	0	25	19	2	1.8	7.9	22	49.3%	.254
2021 FS	HOU	MLB	37	2	2	0	57	0	50	47	7	2.2	8.7	48	45.5%	.293
2021 DC	HOU	MLB	37	2	2	0	53	0	50.7	47	7	2.2	8.7	49	45.5%	.293

Comparables: Jeremy Affeldt, Matt Albers, Justin Speier

Smith's statistics aren't going to tell the story of 2020. There is an absence of information rather than an explanation for his missing numbers. When enough time has passed, readers will be left guessing whether a torn UCL or a global pandemic was responsible for an absent season. We should do our best to remember those, like Smith, who opted out of the season to preserve the health of their loved ones.

YEAR	TEAM	LVL	AGE	WHIP	ERA	DRA-	WARP	MPH	FB%	WHF	CSP
2018	HOU	MLB	34	1.01	3.74	100	0.2	89.4	65.1%	22.4%	
2019	HOU	MLB	35	0.96	1.80	87	0.3	90.0	57.6%	21.2%	
2021 FS	HOU	MLB	37	1.19	3.54	84	0.7	89.7	61.3%	21.8%	53.5%
2021 DC	HOU	MLB	37	1.19	3.54	84	0.7	89.7	61.3%	21.8%	53.5%

Ryne Stanek   RHP
Born: 07/26/91   Age: 29   Bats: R   Throws: R
Height: 6'4"   Weight: 226   Origin: Round 1, 2013 Draft (#29 overall)

YEAR	TEAM	LVL	AGE	W	L	SV	G	GS	IP	H	HR	BB/9	K/9	K	GB%	BABIP
2018	DUR	AAA	26	0	1	2	10	0	9^2	5	1	5.6	15.8	17	58.8%	.250
2018	TB	MLB	26	2	3	0	59	29	66^1	45	8	3.7	11.0	81	32.5%	.253
2019	TB	MLB	27	0	2	0	41	27	55^2	44	7	3.2	9.9	61	30.6%	.264
2019	MIA	MLB	27	0	2	1	22	0	21^1	17	4	8.0	11.8	28	30.8%	.271
2020	MIA	MLB	28	0	0	0	9	0	10	11	3	7.2	9.9	11	34.5%	.308
2021 FS	HOU	MLB	29	2	2	0	57	0	50	42	9	5.0	10.6	58	35.6%	.279
2021 DC	HOU	MLB	29	2	2	0	58	0	50.7	42	9	5.0	10.6	59	35.6%	.279

Comparables: Dominic Leone, Austin Brice, Giovanny Gallegos

Henry Wadsworth Longfellow once wrote a famous poem about ships that pass in the night. Stanek was dealt to Miami in the Nick Anderson deal only a year and a half ago, and at the time he was a more accomplished major-league pitcher than Anderson despite being slightly younger. Since the trade, Anderson has been just about the best reliever in baseball—at least in the regular season—and Stanek has been close to the worst. His career is at risk of disappearing into darkness if he doesn't turn this ship around.

YEAR	TEAM	LVL	AGE	WHIP	ERA	DRA-	WARP	MPH	FB%	WHF	CSP
2018	DUR	AAA	26	1.14	1.86	24	0.4				
2018	TB	MLB	26	1.09	2.98	74	1.4	99.4	60.1%	34.2%	
2019	TB	MLB	27	1.15	3.40	101	0.4	98.9	57.4%	33.7%	
2019	MIA	MLB	27	1.69	5.48	85	0.3	98.6	52.0%	36.9%	
2020	MIA	MLB	28	1.90	7.20	119	0.0	97.2	43.9%	33.7%	
2021 FS	HOU	MLB	29	1.41	4.48	97	0.3	98.8	55.2%	34.4%	42.1%
2021 DC	HOU	MLB	29	1.41	4.48	97	0.4	98.8	55.2%	34.4%	42.1%

Justin Verlander RHP
Born: 02/20/83   Age: 38   Bats: R   Throws: R
Height: 6'5"   Weight: 235   Origin: Round 1, 2004 Draft (#2 overall)

YEAR	TEAM	LVL	AGE	W	L	SV	G	GS	IP	H	HR	BB/9	K/9	K	GB%	BABIP
2018	HOU	MLB	35	16	9	0	34	34	214	156	28	1.6	12.2	290	29.3%	.274
2019	HOU	MLB	36	21	6	0	34	34	223	137	36	1.7	12.1	299	36.1%	.218
2020	HOU	MLB	37	1	0	0	1	1	6	3	2	1.5	10.5	7	61.5%	.091
2021 FS	HOU	MLB	38	3	2	0	57	0	50	39	7	2.2	10.8	59	35.6%	.273

Comparables: A.J. Burnett, John Lackey, Steve Carlton

Pitching until the age of 45 is an ambitious goal for anyone. Verlander seemed a more likely candidate than most to achieve his stated aim. After all, he overcame the injuries and poor performance that accompany many typical mid-30s decline phases and dragged himself back to the pinnacle of the game. Shattering the aging curve is one thing, but doing so with a torn UCL is quite another. That's not to say that pitchers don't come back from Tommy John in their late 30s or beyond; just ask Jamie Moyer. Even Moyer didn't go on to pitch for another half-dozen years afterwards, which is what Verlander will have to do if we're to see him on a major league mound at 45.

YEAR	TEAM	LVL	AGE	WHIP	ERA	DRA-	WARP	MPH	FB%	WHF	CSP
2018	HOU	MLB	35	0.90	2.52	52	7.3	97.1	61.2%	31.9%	
2019	HOU	MLB	36	0.80	2.58	51	7.9	96.6	49.9%	33.7%	
2020	HOU	MLB	37	0.67	3.00	88	0.1	96.6	54.8%	25.7%	
2021 FS	HOU	MLB	38	1.04	2.74	66	1.2	96.8	53.8%	32.9%	49.3%

Forrest Whitley RHP

Born: 09/15/97 Age: 23 Bats: R Throws: R
Height: 6'7" Weight: 238 Origin: Round 1, 2016 Draft (#17 overall)

YEAR	TEAM	LVL	AGE	W	L	SV	G	GS	IP	H	HR	BB/9	K/9	K	GB%	BABIP
2018	CC	AA	20	0	2	0	8	8	26^1	15	2	3.8	11.6	34	37.7%	.220
2019	AST	ROK	21	0	2	0	2	2	4^1	2	0	18.7	20.8	10	50.0%	.333
2019	FAY	HI-A	21	1	0	0	2	2	8^1	4	0	1.1	11.9	11	44.4%	.222
2019	CC	AA	21	2	2	0	6	6	22^2	18	2	7.5	14.3	36	46.7%	.372
2019	RR	AAA	21	0	3	0	8	5	24^1	35	9	5.5	10.7	29	30.7%	.400
2021 FS	HOU	MLB	23	9	9	0	26	26	150	132	27	5.3	10.6	177	37.3%	.292
2021 DC	HOU	MLB	23	4	4	0	12	12	64.7	57	12	5.3	10.6	76	37.3%	.292

Comparables: Julio Urías, Lucas Sims, Jonathan Hernández

Whitley's absence from the majors in 2020 will extend his spell at number one on the Astros prospect list to four consecutive years. It's a run that highlights his top-tier potential and simultaneously veers into prospect fatigue territory, if not sheer exhaustion. The twists and turns of Whitley's journey to the majors didn't stop in the absence of a minor-league campaign. When he arrived at spring training with some considerable extra offseason weight, designed to improve his durability, the team declared he wasn't physically ready to compete for a job. They tinkered with his delivery, resulting in further mechanical changes, some of which Whitley then ditched by the time summer camp rolled around. That wasn't the only thing he lost, as an unconventional diet plan left him rail-thin. After all that, the team seemed positive about his progress and a debut looked imminent—until forearm soreness in early August forced a shutdown. Nothing more serious appears to have come of the issue, and Whitley is still a youthful 23, but with every additional complication one can't help but feel that we might not see the Forrest for the injuries.

YEAR	TEAM	LVL	AGE	WHIP	ERA	DRA-	WARP	MPH	FB%	WHF	CSP
2018	CC	AA	20	0.99	3.76	70	0.6				
2019	AST	ROK	21	2.54	8.31						
2019	FAY	HI-A	21	0.60	2.16	46	0.3				
2019	CC	AA	21	1.63	5.56	112	-0.1				
2019	RR	AAA	21	2.05	12.21	157	-0.2				
2021 FS	HOU	MLB	23	1.47	4.87	106	0.9				
2021 DC	HOU	MLB	23	1.47	4.87	106	0.4				

Astros Prospects

The State of the System:
The Astros have had a long run of success hitting on their OFP 50/55 arms. That will need to continue, because that's most of the system now.

The Top Ten:

1
───────── ★ ★ ★ *2021 Top 101 Prospect* **#69** ★ ★ ★ ─────────
Forrest Whitley   RHP   OFP: 60   ETA: 2021, pending health
Born: 09/15/97   Age: 23   Bats: R   Throws: R   Height: 6'7"   Weight: 238
Origin: Round 1, 2016 Draft (#17 overall)

The Report: As recently as the 2019 Arizona Fall League, Whitley was showing off four plus-or-better offerings: a mid-90s fastball, a diving changeup that tunnels well with the fastball, and two distinct swing-and-miss breakers, a power slider with late tilt and a curveball with strong depth. That AFL stint got us to hold the line on a 70 OFP grade last year despite a woeful regular season. Whitley has struggled with his command and hasn't always had his best stuff coming off injuries; particularly concerning, he's had a string of lat and shoulder issues dating back to 2018. But when he's on, he looks like a top-of-the-rotation starter.

Development Track: Whitley came down with arm soreness during summer camp and wasn't on the mound much in 2020. Ultimately, it was another lost year for the big righty, which particularly stings given all the opportunities that opened up with the big-league club. Although he's yet to suffer any singular particularly serious injury, he just hasn't pitched a whole lot in the last three years, and it's hard to peg him to a particular role until we get a full healthy season.

Variance: High. The No. 2 starter projection is clearly still there somewhere.

J.P. Breen's Fantasy Take: Dynasty owners should always prioritize starters with top-of-the-rotation stuff, and Whitley fits the bill. However, it's hard to justify the righty's current standing as a top-30 dynasty prospect, given his history of injuries, control problems, and bloated ERAs. His dominant appearance in front of scouts in the 2019 AFL has overly inflated his stock, in my mind, as we haven't seen sustained, elite performance since 2017. Given the price tags, I'd rather roll the dice on someone like Michael Kopech. The upside is real, though.

Houston Astros 2021

★ ★ ★ *2021 Top 101 Prospect* **#82** ★ ★ ★

2 Jeremy Peña   SS   OFP: 55   ETA: Late-2021
Born: 09/22/97   Age: 23   Bats: R   Throws: R   Height: 6'0"   Weight: 202
Origin: Round 3, 2018 Draft (#102 overall)

The Report: The 2018 third-rounder was one of 2019's biggest breakout prospects, showing off not just the expected strong defense but surprising offensive skills across both full-season A-ball levels. Peña has strong bat-to-ball abilities and controls the strike zone well. He's never going to be a huge power threat, but he hits the ball in the gaps already and projects to get to at least fringe-average game pop. Defensively, he's a sure-shot shortstop, with better-than-required range, instincts, and arm for the position.

Development Track: Peña was a late addition to the alternate site roster, as Houston took one of the most veteran-heavy groups and only brought in more of their top prospects in September. He got strong reviews for his development there and in instructs, and he's looked very good in the Dominican Winter League so far.

Variance: Medium. We were hoping to see a consolidation season from Peña building on his 2020 breakout, but, well, you know. The circumstantial evidence indicates that he's still on course or perhaps even higher.

J.P. Breen's Fantasy Take: This system gets dynasty-ugly real quick. Peña hit a combined .303/.385/.440 in 2019 with seven homers and 20 stolen bases, and while that's a nice little breakout campaign, it's not exciting in fantasy contexts. The 23-year-old is unlikely to hit for significant power. That puts a lot of pressure on his batting average and stolen bases, and we're not talking about elite skills in either area. We'll need to see another .300-plus season with 20-plus steals before I consider moving him into the top-300 dynasty prospects.

3 Luis Garcia   RHP   OFP: 55   ETA: Debuted in 2020
Born: 12/13/96   Age: 24   Bats: R   Throws: R   Height: 6'1"   Weight: 244
Origin: International Free Agent, 2017

The Report: My biggest miss across our 2020 list product was Luis Garcia. He was in discussion for the Next Ten, but we had a fairly muted report from early in the season on a particularly cold night in the Midwest League. Shortly after the Astros' list went live, I got a text from a scout: "Where was Luis Garcia on your 101?" After figuring out they weren't talking about the Phillies' or Nats' Luis Garcia, I gave a deep sigh and asked for the report. I got back above-average fastball, and the change might be a 70. Yeah, that would explain the 14 K/9 in A-ball. Yes, he was an older signee, but the stuff was advanced, with a full five-pitch mix, featuring three distinct breaking ball looks. The mechanics are a little funky with some deception, which led to some wildness and command scuffles, but Garcia was already built like a major leaguer with the arsenal to match.

Development Track: And he quickly became a major leaguer. The Astros had to lean heavily on their organizational pitching depth in 2020, and Garcia ended up playing a utility arm role for them in September. He pitched well enough to make a playoff roster—and take a playoff start—and the performance didn't look all that out of place for a pitcher with no experience in the upper minors. The fastball can be a bit straight and a bit hittable since Garcia has more control than command at present, but he mixes in the off-speed enough to think he can keep MLB hitters off the fastball. The change has a 10+ mph spread of the fastball and shows big fade and some sink. The slider was more a glove-side chase pitch that didn't always get chases, but the shape of the offering is good and you could see it being above-average with further refinement. I don't know if Garcia fits perfectly as a 180-inning mid-rotation starter, but he's in the right organization to slot in with Framber Valdez andCristian Javier as 130-inning type utility arms who post the rate stats of a good mid-rotation starter That's not quite a Top 101 prospect, but he's certainly on the long list.

Variance: Medium. Garcia pitched well enough in his major-league cameo that he may just slot back into the Astros' 2021 pitching staff in a similar role. A little more minor league time could see him develop into a "real" No. 3 starter, but there is some reliever risk if the fastball remains too hittable across longer outings.

J.P. Breen's Fantasy Take: The 2021 version of Cristian Javier or Jose Urquidy or whoever. The Astros have a ton of these guys. They're useful, but unexciting. Garcia's big-league cameo should make him slightly less available in most dynasty leagues than Javier was 12 months ago. However, he could offer solid rates and volume without costing much on draft day.

4 Alex Santos II   RHP   OFP: 55   ETA: 2025
Born: 02/10/02   Age: 19   Bats: R   Throws: R   Height: 6'3"   Weight: 185
Origin: Round 2, 2020 Draft (#72 overall)

The Report: It's hard enough to draft in a normal year. Add in further complications like a reduction to five rounds—plus losing your first two picks because of the sign-stealing punishment—and the Astros were left with very little opportunity to add to their system. But even with their first pick being 72nd overall, they got a heck of a player in Santos, a right-hander out of the Bronx who was closer to a top-50 talent. With a projectable 6-foot-3 frame paired with an athletic delivery, he fits the mold of the Astros' preferred pitching prospect type, especially when you consider an arsenal that features a high-spin fastball paired with an equally high-spin curveball.

Development Track: Hailing from one of the New York boroughs means baseball season kicks off a little later in the spring, too late for games to begin before the COVID-19 shutdown. Santos was drafted largely off the pedigree from his summer performance the year prior, especially since there had been anticipation to see where a potential velocity spike might have leveled off after winter workouts. The heater still sits in the low 90s while topping out at 96, with many believing he could end up cruising in the mid-to-upper 90s sooner than later. Reports from instructs mentioned his competitive edge despite being the youngest pitcher in camp.

Variance: Very High. Any cold-weather prep pitcher has risk built into their profile. Houston's player development department knows how and whom to identify with a certain set of skills on the mound, and Santos looks like another Jose Urquidy, Cristian Javier, Josh James et al.

J.P. Breen's Fantasy Take: Every organization has one or two high-upside prep pitchers who could pop at any moment. Put him on a 2021 watch list, but don't bother rostering Santos this winter. The lead time is too long, the risk is too high, and there are too many similar arms on the waiver wire every year.

5 Korey Lee C   OFP: 50   ETA: 2023
Born: 07/25/98   Age: 22   Bats: R   Throws: R   Height: 6'2"   Weight: 205
Origin: Round 1, 2019 Draft (#32 overall)

The Report: With the final pick in the first round of the 2019 draft, the Astros surprised many by drafting and then signing Lee to an under-slot deal. Considered by some in the industry as more of a potential third-rounder, Lee's splashy junior year at Cal was undeniably impressive. His slash line improved by nearly 100 points across the board, with his slugging percentage jumping nearly 200 points alone while hitting behind Andrew Vaughn. The raw power flashed plus, but he's unlikely to get to all of it in games while he tries to rework his swing to be less pull-happy. He especially tended to pull off on pitches away. The arm flashes plus as well, even though he wasn't the full-time catcher in college until his junior year, and his raw receiving skills need significant refinement.

Development Track: During his collegiate career, Lee had shown an ability to play multiple positions before settling in solely at catcher. However, upon being drafted, he again was asked to show his versatility by getting time in both left field and first base during his stint in the New York-Penn League. Seldom do you see a first-round catcher—already with limited innings behind the dish—do anything but continue their needed work at the position. This suggests the Astros may value his bat above any defensive value he brings, where he could become a super utility player who can also catch a couple times a week.

Variance: Very High. You had hoped 2020 and a full-season campaign would show evidence of growth both offensively and defensively, instead, we are left with a lot of uncertainty.

J.P. Breen's Fantasy Take: Lee is a more-athletic-than-you-might-think maybe-catcher who would become interesting in fantasy circles if he can develop his skills behind the plate. Think of him like Daulton Varsho, with less speed and an inferior hit tool. In other words, he's a dynasty afterthought for now.

6. Bryan Abreu   RHP   OFP: 50   ETA: Debuted in 2019
Born: 04/22/97   **Age:** 24   **Bats:** R   **Throws:** R   **Height:** 6'1"   **Weight:** 225
Origin: International Free Agent, 2013

The Report: This is an unusually high ranking for a pitcher who broadly falls into the "95-and-a-slider" class of arms. Working in Abreu's favor are two things: (1) It's a really good slider, a potential plus-plus weapon that sits in the mid-80s and touches higher with big two-plane break. (2) He's already pitched in the majors and shown an ability there to miss bats with his stuff. He's also shown issues with command and control, which does limit the upside in the late innings here.

Development Track: Abreu should have been a strong candidate to step into the closer role after the incumbent, Roberto Osuna, tore his UCL shortly into the 2020 season. Abreu showed up to summer camp out of shape though, per *The Athletic*'s Jake Kaplan, and looked more like a "93-and-a-slider" arm who struggled to find the plate. We can't handwave that entirely, but there were going to be some pitchers who struggled to adjust to the unusual start-stop nature of the season, and there's no reason to think Abreu will come into 2021 with the same issues. Well, the control stuff is a little troubling, as even in the minors Abreu's has never been a dart-thrower.

Variance: Medium. Abreu's stuff plays in the bullpen, but how many high-quality strikes he can throw with his stuff will determine the outcome here, which ranges from viable closer to frustrating middle reliever.

J.P. Breen's Fantasy Take: As Mike Gianella has reminded us all offseason, quality middle relievers have underappreciated fantasy value. Abreu has the swing-and-miss stuff to be useful, as shown by his 19.2 percent swinging-strike rate in his big-league debut in 2019, but he'll have to show that he can throw strikes consistently before fantasy owners can trust Abreu to not torpedo their rate stats. The righty is worth a dart throw, though. He might be 2021's Jonathan Hernandez.

7. Freudis Nova   SS   OFP: 50   ETA: 2024
Born: 01/12/00   **Age:** 21   **Bats:** R   **Throws:** R   **Height:** 6'1"   **Weight:** 180
Origin: International Free Agent, 2016

The Report: Despite the seven-figure bonus number, Nova's profile has developed into more of a steady hand as an infield prospect, rather than "seven-figure IFA shortstop prospect." He's played all around the infield the last couple seasons, although he has the physical tools to be an above-average shortstop once he gets more reps at the 6 in higher game speed situations. Nova has struggled against velocity at times despite above-average, whippy bat speed and doesn't project for significant game power. He does enough things well enough that you can squint and see it all come together as a starter in a few years, but given the collection of tools the pro performance so far, you do have to squint a bit.

Development Track: Squint as hard as you want, but you wouldn't have seen much of Nova in 2020. He didn't play at the alternate site; the Astros' camp tilted more toward the major-league-ready. He did spend some time at domestic instructs, but will be 21 next year and yet to play above Low-A, while still needing refinement at shortstop and physical maturation at the plate.

Variance: High. The loss of a potential season of offensive development stings here more than it might other places, given the needed improvements at the plate.

J.P. Breen's Fantasy Take: Some dynasty experts still consider Nova to be a top-300 prospect. In those cases, however, he's still riding the 2018 hype wave, when many (including myself) were enamored with the young infielder. A couple of years later, it's hard to see the impact. Either his approach needs to improve or the power needs to pop. Otherwise, we're looking at a potential utility infielder who is freely available on most big-league waiver wires.

8. Hunter Brown   RHP   OFP: 55   ETA: 2022
Born: 08/29/98   Age: 22   Bats: R   Throws: R   Height: 6'2"   Weight: 203
Origin: Round 5, 2019 Draft (#166 overall)

The Report: Brown was a small college find in the 2019 draft; the Astros popped him out of D2 Wayne State, where he'd only become a regular starting pitcher in his draft year. He was sitting mid-to-upper-90s in the short-season Low-A New York-Penn League after the draft and flashing some interesting secondaries, including a curveball that he added as a pro. But Brown was pitching shorter outings, never even completing three innings, and the command was fringe-at-best, so we had a relief projection on him last year.

Development Track: Our reports highlighted Brown as one of the big risers from instructs, and Jake Kaplan of *The Athletic* reported that he hit 100 mph on a Rapsodo while throwing at home over the summer. It's hard to fully separate the signal from the noise here, because we don't have 2020 live looks and our 2019 post-draft live look wasn't great, but we've got enough overall for the arrow to be pointing up.

Variance: High. It may sound like a broken record here, but we need to see him jump up in a game to fully buy in.

J.P. Breen's Fantasy Take: Brown is one of many pop-up candidates in the lower levels. If he were an offensive player, I'd be interested. Since he's a pitcher, I'll wait and separate the wheat from the chaff in the summer.

9. Colin Barber   OF   OFP: 55   ETA: 2024
Born: 12/04/00   Age: 20   Bats: L   Throws: L   Height: 6'0"   Weight: 185
Origin: Round 4, 2019 Draft (#136 overall)

The Report: The Astros went way, way over-slot to snag Barber as a California prep in the fourth round last year. Early returns are promising; he's a sweet-swinging lefty with a very quick bat and plus power potential. With no minor-league season, he found his way to the City of Champions Cup this summer, a four-team league formed by the independent Joliet Slammers. Barber hit .203/.353/.348 as the youngest player in the league, playing against pitchers who were all far older, many with significant pro track records and a few with big-league time.

Development Track: Barber was invited to the alternate site in September after he played in Joliet, and hit a homer on his first swing in Corpus. Like Brown, Barber was highlighted to us as a player who made a big jump this fall, and the Astros were conservative with alternate site invites and still brought him in, which is a great sign. We're honestly not sure how facing much more advanced pitching than planned is going to influence young hitting prospects; players like Barber got thrown in on the deep end in ways they usually wouldn't have in the pandemic season.

Variance: High. Things are looking quite promising here, but he just turned 20 and hasn't even made his full-season debut yet.

J.P. Breen's Fantasy Take: Folks are always clamoring for the next breakout prospect in the lower levels. That could be Barber in 2021. He's a coveted power-speed type of prospect who few outside of the dynasty diehards have heard about. Don't expect him to ever hit for average, but Barber should be on your supplemental draft board this winter.

10 Jairo Solis   RHP   OFP: 50   ETA: Late-2022 or early-2023
Born: 12/22/99   Age: 21   Bats: R   Throws: R   Height: 6'2"   Weight: 160
Origin: International Free Agent, 2016

The Report: Going back a few years, Solis was on a meteoric rise. He blew through both complex levels and the Appy League in his age-17 season in 2017, and popped up in full-season Low-A the next year at 18 years old. He was extremely, extremely impressive given his age in the Midwest League, with a low-to-mid-90s fastball, a curve flashing plus, and a change flashing above-average. The Astros handled him extremely carefully, reasonably so given his age, with a shortened season and relatively light outings, but he tore his UCL and had Tommy John surgery in the fall anyway. He missed the entire 2019 season, and was still working his way back in 2020.

Development Track: Solis is now fully recovered and ready to go, and he was at fall instructs. He was added to the 40-man roster this offseason, so the option clock is ticking now; we're hoping he picks right back up where he left off.

Variance: Very High. He hasn't pitched competitively in two years and only has 112 pro innings.

J.P. Breen's Fantasy Take: Against my better judgment, I kinda dig Solis. I'd rather take a punt on Solis than Santos or any other non-elite prep hurler. Few non-top-400 have a legit pathway to being a big-league starter. Solis is one of them—though it's far more likely that the Astros develop him into one of their 120-inning swingman types.

The Prospects You Meet Outside The Top Ten

MLB-Ready Arms, But Less Upside Than You'd Like

Shawn Dubin   RHP   Born: 09/06/95   Age: 25   Bats: R   Throws: R   Height: 6'1"   Weight: 154   Origin: Round 13, 2018 Draft (#402 overall)
Dubin stood out as one of the few prospects to be invited to summer camp initially who didn't have upper-level minors experience; he pitched most of 2019 in High-A. He didn't make it to the majors even as the Astros rotated through a lot of arms (an early unexplained IL stint set him back), but he was on the postseason taxi squad. The lanky righty has bat-missing stuff, led by a mid-90s fastball and tough slider, but might not have the frame to start long term.

Austin Hansen   RHP   Born: 08/25/96   Age: 24   Bats: R   Throws: R   Height: 6'0"   Weight: 195   Origin: Round 8, 2018 Draft (#252 overall)
Hansen is maybe the most obvious reliever of this group, although he was still used within the Astros' tandem starting model in 2019. The 2018 eighth rounder was a dominant reliever for Oklahoma in college, and while the Astros stretched him back out, the whirling dervish, high effort delivery will work best in short bursts, where his fastball might play into the upper-90s and complement two power breakers he can use to miss bats.

Peter Solomon   RHP   Born: 08/16/96   Age: 24   Bats: R   Throws: R   Height: 6'4"   Weight: 201   Origin: Round 4, 2017 Draft (#121 overall)
Solomon's elbow blew out very early in the 2019 season and he ended up undergoing Tommy John surgery. Like Solis, he's now recovered and should be a full go for the 2021 season, and was added to the 40-man roster in the offseason. Back in 2018, the 2017 fourth-rounder out of Notre Dame profiled with a mid-90s fastball and advanced secondaries led by a quality breaker; he could move quickly once back in games, but the elbow surgery increases the reliever risk here.

Tyler Ivey   RHP   Born: 05/12/96   Age: 25   Bats: R   Throws: R   Height: 6'4"   Weight: 195   Origin: Round 3, 2017 Draft (#91 overall)

Hmm, the Astros sure seem to like righties with unorthodox, often effortful mechanics and multiple breaking ball looks (to be fair, they also like lefties like that). Ivey is another in this group with mid-90s heat and two useable breaking balls. Like Hansen, the mechanics portend a move to the pen, where Ivey could fill a setup or multi-inning role.

MLB-Ready Bat, But Less Upside Than You'd Like

Chas McCormick   RF   Born: 04/19/95   Age: 26   Bats: R   Throws: L   Height: 6'0"   Weight: 208   Origin: Round 21, 2017 Draft (#631 overall)

McCormick was a Day 3, Division II senior sign outfielder, who paved a fairly non-descript path to the upper minors. He was always old for his levels, but also always hit enough that he'd have to find a new apartment in a new town around mid-season. Then McCormick hit enough at the alternate site in 2020 to find himself a surprise playoff roster addition, although that was more likely due to his speed. He's never hit for much power outside of the 2019 PCL, but there's maybe a bit more game power than Myles Straw, and the plus speed and approach might make him a useful bench outfielder in that type of mold.

Top Talents 25 and Under (as of 4/1/2021):

1. Kyle Tucker, OF
2. Yordan Alvarez, DH/OF
3. Forrest Whitley, RHP
4. Jose Urquidy, RHP
5. Cristian Javier, RHP
6. Jeremy Peña, SS
7. Luis Garcia, RHP
8. Alex Santos, RHP
9. Abraham Toro, 3B
10. Korey Lee, C

After several years of coming just short of fully breaking through, Kyle Tucker settled in as a very good major-league regular in 2020. As Houston's regular left fielder (occasionally flipping over to right), he put up a 116 DRC+ in his age-23 season, and he hit fifth or sixth in every playoff game. We think there's even better to come from his talented lefty bat.

It's very difficult to place Yordan Alvarez in context right now. Just six months ago, it would've been unthinkable to put him behind Tucker, but there he is. Alvarez only played in two games in 2020 amid injuries to both knees that started in spring training, and he had surgery on both in August after tearing his right patella tendon. He's an offensive force when healthy, but there's a lot of uncertainty now.

2019 breakout star Urquidy missed much of the 2020 season with COVID-19. When he came back, he looked like the Urquidy of 2019 again, 92-94 with a plus changeup and the occasional deadly slider. He looked solid in the postseason, and is probably just a present mid-rotation type, albeit with a bit more risk since he still only has 12 regular-season MLB starts.

Coming into the season, we had Cristian Javier projected with some serious bullpen risk, but he took a regular turn in Houston's rotation and ended up netting a third place in AL Rookie of the Year voting. The righty mostly works off a low-90s fastball and a slurvy breaker, with the occasional changeup mixed in. He was effective in the playoffs shifted to a multi-inning role, and that was closer to the projection we had on him last year. But right now he looks like a present third or fourth starter with a bit of upside past that.

Abraham Toro stuck on the Astros roster in 2020, albeit in a backup role. He saw semi-regular time when Alex Bregman was injured and filled in a bit as a reserve corner infielder when Bregman was healthy. He hit poorly in a small sample— a .149 batting average and 80 DRC+—but we still see him as a well-rounded future regular overall.

Part 3: Featured Articles

Astros All-Time Top 10 Players

by Matthew Trueblood

POSITION PLAYERS

JEFF BAGWELL, 1B (1991-2005)
The relative brevity of his career (thanks to a brutal shoulder injury) and unsourced, unsubstantiated allegations of PED use have stopped Bagwell from being compared favorably to the other potential claimants for the title of "Best First Baseman Ever," but he has a strong case. He developed an extraordinarily good batting eye, stole bases in greater volume and at a higher success rate than almost any other first baseman in history, and played terrific defense, despite being relatively short for the spot. At the plate, his deep crouch, padded batting gloves, wild chin beard, and lethal swing were as evocative as his numbers were impressive.

JOE MORGAN, 2B (1963-1971, 1980)
Oversimplified narratives of history might lead one to think that Morgan only found himself and blossomed into a superstar after he was traded to Cincinnati. He did find far better power there, having escaped the Astrodome, but his incredible patience, contact skills, and speed were on full display even while in Houston. But for the racism of manager Harry Walker, Morgan might have thrived in Houston and become the team's first Hall of Famer.

BILL DORAN, 2B, (1982-1990)
A darling of the nascent sabermetric movement, Doran walked a lot, rarely struck out, and was far more valuable than his tepid batting averages implied. That didn't mean he was a secret superstar; he lacked the power, the defensive ability, and the baserunning efficiency for that. He just piled up workmanlike seasons of well-rounded, above-average performance.

CRAIG BIGGIO, 2B/C/OF (1988-2007)

Famous for refusing to clean the pine tar off his helmet between games and thus letting the stuff cake up over the season, Biggio understood his brand. He was all hustle and slides and dirt and scrapes (some of them more style than substance). He had uncommon power for his position and for a leadoff hitter, but never wanted to bat anywhere else. He pioneered the wearing of heavy padding that allowed him to gleefully accept free trips to first base if pitchers worked him inside. At his best, he hit for high averages, added value with his legs, and was a passable fielder at multiple positions. Among players who debuted after integration, only Pete Rose and Albert Pujols have more doubles. The only regrettable aspect of all this was the quest for 3,000 hits that kept him on the field well past the point of diminishing returns; there's no "3,000" in "team."

JOSÉ ALTUVE, 2B, 2011-PRESENT

Scouts nearly refused to watch the Lilliputian Altuve work out for them when he was a teenager in Venezuela. They were right to believe he would never grow big enough to appear to belong on a big-league field, but wrong to think that would matter. With supernal feel to hit and plenty of speed, Altuve shot through the minor leagues, and it quickly became evident that he had untapped power potential, too. He's now a stocky, slugging former MVP, and even if a down 2020 and the cloud of the cheating scandal still hang over him, it's impossible not to be impressed by Altuve's drive to improve and succeed.

JIM WYNN, OF (1963-1973)

Wynn was not only short, but slightly built, earning him the nickname "The Toy Cannon" and leading some to underestimate his presence in the batter's box and beyond. His play commanded respect, though, and the sobriquet became more about "Cannon" and less about "Toy." Wynn traded contact for power but generated a staggering amount of it despite his size. Extremely selective and unwilling to cut down his swing, he sometimes ran low batting averages which led him to be underrated later in his career, but he could do it all. He was Houston's first homegrown star.

CÉSAR CEDEÑO, OF (1970-1981)

There have been only a handful of players in modern history who have been above-average regulars at age 19. Cedeño is on that short list, and throughout his 20s, he was a dazzling player. For his era, and adjusting for the effects of the Astrodome, he had very good power, but most of it came in the form of doubles. He really stood out with his speed, with an average of 43 steals (and just 13 times caught) over his first 11 seasons. He faded quickly thereafter but his peak was electrifying.

JOSÉ CRUZ, OF (1975-1987)

To see Cruz's full value, you have to pull back and apply soft focus, like you're trying to see the hidden picture in a maze of colorful geometrics. He wasn't dominant in any area, and some of his best skills were slightly rough-edged. He was fast but didn't steal bases as efficiently as one might dream. He played good defense but was confined to the outfield corners for most of his career. Try to look through the individual shapes, though, and an impressive tableau emerges: the lefty-swinging Cruz hit for slightly above-average power, consistently got hits on balls in play, walked more than an average hitter, and struck out less. His abilities might have been more obvious had not appeared to be a bust in his first major league trial (with the Cardinals, who flat sold him to the Astros) and if he had played anywhere but the Astrodome at its most abstemious, although he hit well there, averaging .297/.372/.423 there as an Astro,

TERRY PUHL, OF (1977-1990)

In 1980, Cruz, Cedeño, and the Canadian Puhl became the first trio of foreign-born outfielders ever to qualify for the batting title on the same team. They played together for some time, though injuries, platoons, and trades made the relationship inconstant. Puhl was another player with more balance than brilliance to his game: he had very little power but made pitchers work, put the ball in play, and used good speed and bat control to hit for respectable averages. A sure glove who went whole seasons, without making an error, Puhl moved all over the outfield but consistently acquitted himself well.

LANCE BERKMAN, OF/1B (1999-2010)

To get Berkman out you had to throw him all three strikes. Even then, your odds weren't great. He was a switch-hitter, and although he was only truly dominant against righties, his superb batting eye worked from either side of the plate. He had a very compact, uppercut swing, especially as a lefty, generating easy power without sacrificing much contact. A beer-league build made him unhelpful on the bases and in the field, but a career OBP of .406 more than made up for those shortcomings.

PITCHERS

LARRY DIERKER, RHP (1964-1976)

In today's game, the four-seamer and the sinker are fully distinct pitches. Pitchers throw one or the other or use them in distinct ways and situations. Dierker, however, would start a game with both heaters at his fingertips, see which was working better for him that day, and then hew to it the rest of the way. He also had an often-devastating forkball, though he wasn't able to throw it well after a pickup basketball injury about halfway through his career. He debuted on his 18th birthday but was out of baseball shortly after his 31st.

DON WILSON, RHP (1966-1974)

Wilson's fastball was explosive—maybe the best of an era in which there were many famous, dominant fastballs. He threw it very hard, but the late movement on the pitch made it truly special. It sometimes sailed, and he could miss bats at the top of the zone. It sometimes sank, running to the arm side. Still other times, it acted as what we would now call a power cutter, still in the mid-90s, but with the ability to skid away from righties or into the hands of lefties. It was that heat that let Wilson throw two no-hitters, strike out 18 in a game, and post 6.7 WARP in 1971. His death, at age 29 in early 1975, is a deeply tragic story, though one that goes far beyond the diamond.

KEN FORSCH, RHP (1970-1980)

Forsch was a fine but fungible starter at each end of his career. For half a decade in the middle he became the Astros' fireman, and could be dominant. With a slider and a forkball that drew weak contact and kept the ball in the park, he averaged 105 innings and had a 2.73 ERA from 1974-1978, serving as everything from a starter to a closer.

J.R. RICHARD, RHP (1971-1980)

Even better than Wilson had been at his best, Richard was working on a Hall of Fame-caliber peak when he was forced out of the game. Built like a power forward, Richard was an overpowering pitcher. Few pitchers in history have thrown as hard a true slider; hitters had no chance, when he had command of it. The stroke he suffered on a July day in 1980 set him on a tragic path, not only ending his career but starting a spiral that led him to homelessness. Heroically, he survived and regained his footing.

JOE NIEKRO, RHP (1975-1985)

The full career track record of the lesser Niekro knuckleballer is mixed, but during his decade-plus with the Astros, he was quite good. His knuckler never missed enough bats to allow him to dominate, and he had even worse control problems than some other artisans of the craft, but he managed top-five Cy Young finishes in 1979 and 1980. Late in his Houston career, he led the league with 38 starts in consecutive seasons.

NOLAN RYAN, RHP (1980-1988)

Incomparable. Ryan had unmatched endurance, terrific stuff, and, at first, no control whatsoever. He cut his walk rate from 5.4 per nine with the Angels to 3.9 with the Astros, a step towards efficiency that helped keep him pitching until he was 46. Ryan pitched at least 500 innings for each of the four teams for whom he pitched, so he doesn't belong to any one team, but both of his career ERA titles came with Houston. It was his nine-year Astros tenure, too, which bridged into his 40s, that proved he could outlast even the other pitchers who might have seemed to be similarly durable. His 1987, when he led the NL in ERA and strikeouts but went 8-16 due to a complete lack of offensive support would have made for a fascinating test of post-millennium Cy Young Award voters woke to the externalities that affect pitcher won-lost records.

MIKE SCOTT, RHP (1983-1991)

In 1986, Scott was not only the NL Cy Young Award winner, but a historic powerhouse. With what hitters repeatedly insisted (probably correctly) was a splitter artificially enhanced by scuffing the ball, Scott led the league in ERA, innings, strikeouts, and WHIP. He enjoyed a half-decade or so of dominance, thanks in large part to the splitter, though he was fairly pedestrian both before and after that window.

SHANE REYNOLDS, RHP (1992-2002)

If you believe in our Deserved Run Average models, Reynolds is one of history's most underrated hurlers, and a diamond disguised as mere coal by the combination of expansion and some bad defenses behind him. His career FIP of 3.63 bested his ERA by half a run, but DRA goes even further: from 1995-99, DRA-based Wins Above Replacement Player credits Reynolds with over 36 wins of value, more than Roger Clemens had over the same span.

ROY OSWALT, RHP (2001-2010)

In an age of big, strapping starting pitchers, Oswalt was a short, skinny one. Yet, he threw fiercely hard, in his youth, and even as his velocity declined, he had good life on his fastballs, be they riding four-seamers or sinkers. His curveball, an old-fashioned one that often had 20 miles per hour of separation from his heat, kept batters honest, and he could throw it either for called strikes or into the dirt to draw a chase. Aggressive and unwilling to issue free passes lightly, he nonetheless limited hard contact. Most surprisingly of all, perhaps, despite his frame, Oswalt was a workhorse for a solid decade, mostly on very good Astros teams.

DALLAS KEUCHEL, LHP (2012-2018)

Never a hard thrower, Keuchel has always lived on the edges of the zone. In fact, at his best, he had the lowest aggregate Called Strike Probability of any starter in baseball. He dominated by demonstrating excellent command, getting help from the Astros' great pitch-framers, and trusting the aggressively shifted defenses behind him—and with a heavy, well-paired sinker-slider-changeup arsenal.

A Taxonomy of 2020 Abnormalities

by Rob Mains

I'm going to start this with a trivia question. Trust me, it's relevant. Don't bother skipping to the end of the article to find the answer, it's not there.

Only five players have appeared in 140 or more games for 16 straight seasons. Who are they?

It's a trivia question starting off an essay, so you know how this works: Whatever you guessed, you're wrong. It's okay. As someone who purchased this book, chances are good that you're an educated baseball fan. But the circumstances behind 2020 force us to abandon, or at least seriously question, some of our favorite patterns and crutches for evaluating the game we love.

We just completed what was undoubtedly the strangest season in MLB history. No fans, geographically limited schedule, universal DH, seven-inning twin bills, runners on second in extra innings, a 16-team postseason, a club playing at a Triple-A stadium. Some of these changes will likely persist (sorry), but we've never had so many tweaks dumped on us all at once, at least not since they figured out how many balls were in a walk.

And the biggest, of course, was the 60-game season. The 19th century was dotted with teams that went bankrupt before the season ended, but the lone season with only 60 scheduled games was 1877. That year there were only six teams, the league rostered a total of 77 players (just 16 more than the 2020 Marlins), and batters called for pitches to be thrown high or low by the pitcher, who was 50 feet away. We can say the 2020 season was easily the shortest ever for recognizable baseball.

As such, it'll stand out. Few abbreviated seasons do. Just about everybody reading this knows the 1994 season ended after Seattle's Randy Johnson struck out Oakland's Ernie Young for the last out of the Mariners-A's game on August 11. The ensuing player strike wiped out the rest of the season and the postseason. Teams played only 112-117 games that year.

And many of you know that a strike in the middle of the 1981 season split the season in two, resulting in the only Division Series until 1995. Teams played only 103-111 games that year, the shortest regular season since 1885.

Those two seasons are memorable. So when we see that nobody drove in 100 runs in 1981, or that Greg Maddux was the only pitcher with 180 or more innings pitched in 1994, we think, "Of course. Strike year."

But we don't remember other short years. You might not recall that the 1994 strike spilled into the next year, chopping 18 games off the 1995 schedule. You might've read that the 1918 season, played during the last pandemic, ended after Labor Day due to the government's World War I "work or fight" order. A strike erased the first week and a half of the 1972 season, but that year's best known as the last time pitchers batted in the American League.

The point is, while we don't remember small changes to the schedule, we remember the big ones. The 1981 mid-season strike. The 1994 season- and Series-ending strike. And, of course, the pandemic-shortened 2020 season. We won't need a reminder why Marcell Ozuna's 18 homers were the fewest to lead the National League in a century. (Literally; Cy Williams led with 15 in 1920.)

Now, about that trivia question. The five players are Hank Aaron, Brooks Robinson, Pete Rose, Ichiro Suzuki, and Johnny Damon. The one nobody gets, of course, is Damon, and a lot of people miss Ichiro, whose last season of 140-plus games came garbed in the red-orange and ocean blue of Miami when he was 42. That's half of what makes it a good question. The other half is the two guys whom many think made the list but didn't. Lou Gehrig? His streak started in the Yankees' 42nd game of the 1925 season and lasted only 13 seasons after that. And everybody assumes Cal Ripken Jr. did it, having played 2,632 straight games over 17 seasons. But one of those 17 seasons was 1994, when the Orioles played only 112 games.

My point? *I just told you* everybody remembers the 1994 strike year, but everybody forgets it fell in the middle of Ripken's streak, separating the first twelve years from the last four. Just because we recall something doesn't mean it's always at the front of our minds.

Nobody is going to forget 2020, and baseball is obviously not the main reason. But there will come a time in the future when you're looking at a player's or a team's record, and there will be baffling numbers there for 2020, and you'll think, "I wonder what happened." (Not to mention the missing line for minor league players.) Just like you forgot that the 1994 strike limited Ripken to 112 games.

Try not to forget it, though. The 2020 season resulted in weird statistical results for several reasons.

There were only 60 games.
I know, duh. But that had impacts beyond counting stats like Ozuna's home run total or Yu Darvish and Shane Bieber leading the majors with eight wins. (I know, pitcher wins, but still.)

The 162-game season is the longest among major North American sports, and that duration gives us a gift. Over the course of a long season, small variations tend to even out. A player who has a ten-game hot streak will probably have a ten-game cold streak. A team that starts the year losing a bunch of close games will probably win a bunch of them. We get regression to the mean. Statistics stabilize.

Consider flipping a coin. Over the long run, we expect it to come up heads about half the time. But the fewer flips, the more variation there'll be. If you flip a coin six times, probability theory tells us you'll get at least two-third heads about 34 percent of the time. Flip it 30 times, your chance of two-thirds heads drops to five percent.

Or, relevant to this case, if you flip a coin 60 times, your chance of getting at least 36 heads—that's 60 percent—is 7.75 percent. Expand the coin-flipping to 162 times, and the chance of getting 60 percent heads drops to 0.73 percent.

In other words, the odds of an outcome that's 20 percent better (or worse) than expected is *more than ten times higher* when you flip your coin 60 times than when you do it 162 times. Call it small sample size, call lack of mean reversion, or call it luck not evening out, 162 is a lot more predictive than 60. You get much more variation over 60 games than over 162. Bieber's 1.63 ERA and 0.87 FIP aren't something we'd see over a full season, and neither is Javier Baéz's .203/.238/.360.

Some players' lines in 2020 look normal. Brian Anderson had an .811 OPS in 2019 and an .810 OPS in 2020. (He probably would have gotten that last point if he'd been given enough time.) But there are many like Bieber and Baéz, some of them from young players still establishing their talent levels. The answer to the question, "What went right or wrong for that guy in 2020?" is most likely "Nothing, it was just a 2020 thing."

Preseason training was abbreviated for hitters.

Every year, spring training drags. Players get tired of it, fans get tired of it, and you sure can tell sportswriters get tired of it. Yes, something to get everyone into shape is necessary, but does it really have to drag on for over a month? Can't we shorten it?

The 2020 season answered in the negative, at least for hitters. Warren Spahn is credited with saying that hitting is timing and pitching is upsetting timing. It appears nobody had his timing down after the abbreviated July summer camp. Through August 9—18 games into the season—MLB batters were hitting .230/.311/.395 with a .275 BABIP. That BABIP, had it held, would have been the lowest since 1968, the Year of the Pitcher. In recent years it's hovered around .300.

It didn't hold. Play returned to more normal levels the rest of the year: .249/.325/.425 with a .297 BABIP starting August 10. But batters whose play concentrated in those first two weeks wound up with ugly lines. Andrew

Benintendi went on the injured list with a season-ending rib cage strain on August 11. His final line: .103/.314/.128 in 14 games. Franchy Cordero went on the IL with a hamate bone fracture on August 9 and a .154/.185/.231 line. Even though he came back strong in a late September return, it was too late to repair his full-season numbers.

Preseason training was abbreviated for pitchers.
Every year, spring training drags. Players get tired of it, fans get tired of it … wait, I already said that. But the abbreviated preseason was tough on pitchers, too. As noted, they had the upper hand coming out of the gate. But then they lost that hand. And then their arms, too.

The 2020 season was spread over 67 days. During those 67 days, 237 pitchers hit the Injured List, compared to 135 in the first 67 days of 2019. A lot of those IL stints, though, were COVID-19-related. Still, over the first 67 days of the 2019 season, there were 72 pitchers on the IL with arm injuries. That figure jumped to 110 in 2020, a 53 percent increase.

There are a number of factors contributing to pitcher arm injuries, ranging from usage to velocity, but it appears that attenuated preseason training played a role. A lot of pitchers had super-short seasons due to arm woes. Corey Kluber, Roberto Osuna, and Shohei Ohtani combined for seven innings, none after August 8. All suffered arm injuries. We'll never know whether they'd have fared better with a longer preseason, but we can guess how they probably feel.

Everybody played.
Rosters were set to expand from 25 to 26 in 2020, so even if we'd had a normal season, we'd have likely seen 2019's record of 1,410 players on MLB rosters broken. But due to the pandemic, rosters started the year at 30 and were cut to only 28. Add multiple COVID-19 absences and the revolving door caused by poor starts by hitters and a rash of pitcher arm injuries, and 1,289 players appeared in MLB games in 2020. The comparable figure over the first 67 days of the 2019 season was 1,109. That 16 percent increase works out to an average of six more players per team in 2020 compared to a similar slice of 2019. A future look back at 2020 rosters will include a lot of unfamiliar names.

Plus became a minus.
In advanced metrics, we adjust batter and pitcher performance for park and league/era variations. A plus sign appended to the end of a measure means that it's adjusted for park and league. It's scaled to an average of 100, with higher figures above average and lower figures below average. (Similarly, a metric with a minus is also park- and league-adjusted and scaled to 100, with lower values better.) Here at BP, our advanced measure of offensive performance is DRC+. Baseball-Reference has OPS+ and FanGraphs has wRC+.

Using park and league adjustments, we can compare Dante Bichette's 1995 Steroid Era season at pre-humidor Coors Field (.340/.364/.620, 40 homers, 128 RBI, MVP runner-up) with Jim Wynn's 1968 Year of the Pitcher season at the cavernous Astrodome (.269/.376/.474, 26 homers, 67 RBI, no MVP votes). It's not close. DRC+, OPS+, and wRC+ all give the nod to Wynn, handily. This is a useful tool. As my Baseball Prospectus colleague Patrick Dubuque tweeted last fall, "Please note that when I ask how you are, I am already adjusting for era."

The 2020 season messes up plus (and minus) stats for two reasons. First, the park adjustment was based on only 30 home games instead of the usual 81. Everything noted above regarding the short season applies, literally doubly, to park effect calculations. DRC+ uses a single-season park factor. OPS+ uses a three-year average and wRC+ five years. The figure for 2020 is suspect.

Second, OPS+ and wRC+ adjust for league: American and National. (DRC+ adjusts for opponent, regardless of league.) While there were two leagues in 2020, they were an artificial construct. To reduce travel, teams played opponents geographically, not based on league. There weren't two leagues, American and National. There were three, Western, Central, and Eastern.

That makes a difference because teams in the same league played in different run-scoring environments. AL teams scored 4.58 runs per game, NL teams 4.71. That's a small difference. But teams in the East scored 0.21 more runs per game (4.95) than teams in the West (4.74), and they both scored a lot more than Central teams (4.25). Adjusting for league misses that difference, so this book will be safe in that regard, but other sources may be distorted somewhat.

Not every game was a "game."
In 2020, the rising tide of strikeouts was finally stemmed. Strikeouts per team per game fell from 8.8 in 2019 to 8.7 in 2020. That marked the first decline after 14 straight annual increases.

In 2020, the rising tide of strikeouts rose higher. Batters struck out in 23.4 percent of plate appearances compared to 23.0 percent in 2019. That marked the 15th straight annual increase.

Both are true statements.

Because of two rule changes—seven-inning doubleheaders and runners on second in extra innings—games in 2020 were unprecedented in their brevity. There were 37.0 plate appearances per game in 2020. The only years with fewer were 1904 and 1906-1909. The average game in 2020 entailed 8.61 innings pitched, the fewest since 1899.

So when you see any per-game stats for 2020, you need to increase them by 3 or 4 percent to get them on equal footing with recent years.

Or, better, just ignore them. Last year happened. There were major league games contested between major league teams. But when you're looking at those physical or electronic baseball cards, when you're weaving narratives over why this young player's inevitable rise to stardom fell apart or why that old veteran rekindled his magic, don't linger on the 2020 line. It was just too weird.

Thanks to Lucas Apostoleris for research assistance.

—Rob Mains is an author of Baseball Prospectus.

Tranches of WAR

by Russell A. Carleton

We ask "replacement level" to be a lot of things. Sometimes contradictory things. Sometimes I wonder if we know what it even means anymore. The original idea was that it represented the level of production that a team could expect to get from "freely available talent", including bench players, minor leaguers, and waiver wire pickups. It created a common benchmark to compare everyone to, and for that reason, it represented an advancement well beyond what was available at the time. In fact, it created a language and a framework for evaluating players that was not just better but *entirely* different than what came before it.

But then we started mumbling in that language. The idea behind "wins above replacement" was one part sci-fi episode and one part mathematical exercise. Imagine that a player had disappeared before the season and suddenly, in an alternate timeline, his team would have had to replace him. The distance between him and that replacement line was his value. We need to talk about that alternate timeline.

Without getting too into 2:00 am "deep conversations" with extensive navel-gazing, it's worth thinking about why one player might not be playing, while another might.

- A player might not be playing because he has a short-term injury or his manager believes that he needs a day off.
- A player might not be playing because he has a longer-term injury that requires him to be on the injured list.

There's a difference here between these two situations. In particular, the first one generally *doesn't* involve a compensatory roster move, while the second one does. It's possible, though not guaranteed, that the person who will be replacing the injured/resting player would be the same in either case. That matters. Teams generally carry a spare part for all eight position players on the diamond, although in the era of a four-player bench, those spare parts usually are the backup plan for more than one spot.

A couple of years ago, I posed a hypothetical question. Suppose that a team had two players in its system fighting for a fourth outfielder spot. One of them was a league average hitter, but would be worth 20 runs below average if allowed to play center field for a full season. One of them was a perfectly average fielder, but would be 15 runs below average as a hitter, if allowed to play an entire season. Which of the two should the team roster? It's tempting to say the second one, as overall, he is the better player. That misses the point. A league average hitter on the bench isn't just a potential replacement for an injured outfielder. He might also pinch hit for the light-hitting shortstop in a key spot. You keep the average hitter on the roster, even though he isn't a hand-in-glove fit for one specific place on the field, because being a bench player is a different job description than being a long-term fill-in for someone. If you find yourself in need of a longer-term fill-in, you can bring the other guy up from AAA.

When we're determining the value of an everyday player though, if he had disappeared before the season and a team would have had to replace his production, they likely would have done it with a player who was a long-term fill-in type because they would have had to replace a guy who played everyday. Maybe that's the same guy that they would have rostered on their bench anyway, but we don't know. It gets to the query of what we hope to accomplish with WAR. Are we looking for an accurate modeling of reality or are we looking for a common baseline to compare everyone to? Both have their uses, but they are somewhat different questions.

Let's talk about another dichotomy.

- A player might not be playing because he isn't very good and is a bench-level player.
- A player might not be playing because there is another player on the team who has a situational advantage that makes him the better choice today. The classic case of this is a handedness platoon. On another day, he might be a better choice.

When we think about player usage, I think we're still stuck in the model that there are starters and there are scrubs. We have plenty of words for bench players or reserves or backups or utility guys. We do still have the word "platoon" in our collective vocabulary, but in the age of short benches, it's hard to construct one. It's always been hard to construct them. You have to find two players who hit with different hands, have skill sets that complement each other, and probably play the same position. In the era of the short bench, one of them had probably better double as a utility player in some way. Baseball has a two-tiered language geared toward the idea of regulars and reserves. The fact that it was so easy for me to find plenty of synonyms for "a player whose primary function is to come into a game to replace a regular player if he is injured or resting" should tell you something.

I'm always one to look for "unspoken words" in baseball. What is it called when someone is both half of a platoon and the utility infielder? That guy exists sometimes, but he reveals himself in that role—usually by accident. We don't have a word for that, and whenever I find myself saying "we don't have a word for that", I look for new opportunities. What do you call it, further, when the job of being the utility infielder is decentralized across the whole infield with occasional contributions from the left fielder? It's not even a "super-utility" player. What happens when you build your entire roster around the idea that everyone will be expected to be a triple major?

⚾ ⚾ ⚾

I think someone else beat me to this one, and on a grand scale. Platoons work because we know that hitters of the opposite hand to the pitcher get better results than hitters of the same hand, usually to the tune of about 20 points of OBP. If you want to express that in runs, it usually comes out to somewhere around 10 to 12 runs of linear weights value prorated across 650 PA. But hang on a second, now let's say that we have two players who might start today, both of roughly equal merit with the bat. One has a handedness advantage, but is the worse fielder of the two. In that case, as long as his "over the course of a season" projection as a fielder at whatever position you want to slot him into is less than a 10-run drop from the guy he might replace, then he's a better option today.

We're not used to thinking of utility players as bat-first options, who would play below-average defense at three different infield positions. That guy might hook on as a 2B/3B/LF type (Howie Kendrick, come on down!) but teams usually think to themselves that they need as their utility infielder someone who "can handle" shortstop, the toughest of the infield spots to play. If someone can do that *and* hit well, he's probably already starting somewhere, so he's not available as a utility infielder. It's easier for those glove guys to find a job. In a world where the replacement for a shortstop *has to be* the designated utility infielder, that makes sense.

But as we talked about last week, we're living in a different world. The rate at which a replacement for a regular starter turns out to be *another starter* shifting over to cover has gone way up over the last five years. There was always some of it in the game, but this has been a supernova of switcheroos. Now if your second baseman is capable of playing a decent shortstop, that 2B/3B/LF guy can swap in. He's not actually playing shortstop, and maybe the defense suffers from the switch, but if he's got enough of a bat, he might outhit those extra fielding miscues. And in doing so, he is effectively your backup shortstop.

Somewhere along the lines, teams got hip to the idea of multi-positional play from their regulars. I've written before about how you can't just put a player, however athletic, into a new position and expect much at first. The data tell us that. Eventually, players can learn to be multi-positionalists, but it takes time, roughly on the order of two months, before they're OK. But there's a hidden message in there. If you give a player some reps at a new spot, he's a reasonably gifted athlete and somewhat smart and willing to learn, he could probably pick it up enough to get to "good enough," and it doesn't take forever. You just have to be purposeful about it. Maybe you get to the point where you can start to say "he's still below average but we could move him there and get another bat into the lineup, and it's a net win."

Teams have started to build those extra lessons into their player development program. It used to be seen as a mark of weakness to be relegated to "utility player" because that meant that you were a bench player (all those synonyms above come with a side of stigma). Now, it's a way of building a team. If you get a few reps in the minors (where it doesn't count) at a spot, you'll have at least played the spot at game speed before. There are limits to how far you can push that. A slow-footed "he's out in left field because we don't have the DH" guy is never going to play short, but maybe your third baseman can try second base and not look like a total moose out there.

⚾ ⚾ ⚾

Back to WAR. I'd argue that the world of starters and scrubs is slowly disintegrating, for good cause. In the event that a regular starter really does go down with an injury–ostensibly, the alternate universe scenario that WAR is attempting to model–it makes the team a little more resilient to replacing him. And the good news is that you're more likely to be able to replace him with the best of the bench bunch, rather than the third-best guy, because the best guy doesn't have to be an exact positional match for the guy who got hurt. And that's what the manager would want to do. He'd want to replace that long-term production, not with an amalgam of everyone else who played that position, but with the best guy available from his reserves.

Now this is still WAR. We still want to retain the principle that we should be measuring a player, and not his teammates. We need some sort of common baseline, and despite what I just said, we'll still need some sort of amalgam. To construct that, I give to you the idea of the tranche. The word, if you've not heard it before, refers to a piece of a whole that is somehow segmented off. It's often used in finance to talk about layers of a financial instrument.

Here, I want you to consider that there are 30 starters at each of the seven non-battery positions (catchers should have their own WAR, since only a catcher can replace a catcher). We can identify them by playing time, and we can futz around with the definition a little bit if we need to. Next, among those who aren't in that starting pool, we identify the top tranche of the 30 best bench players, which I would again identify by playing time, and then the second and third and fourth and so on. If a player were to disappear, his manager would probably want to take a guy from that top tranche of the bench to replace him. In a world where even the starters can slide around the field, that becomes more feasible.

We can take a look at that top tranche and say "How many of them showed that they are able to play (first, second, etc.)?" and therefore could have directly substituted for the starter? How many of them could have been a direct substitute for our injured player? We don't know whether one of them would be on *a specific* team, but we can say that 40 percent of the time, a manager would have been able to draw from tranche 1 in filling the role, and 35 percent from tranche 2. But on tranche 1, we can also look at how many of those players played a position that could have then shifted and covered for that spot. We'd need some eligibility criteria for all of this (probably a minimum number of games played) but it would just be a matter of multiplication. Shortstop would be harder to fill, and managers would probably be dipping a little further down in the talent pool, and so replacement level would be lower, as it is now.

Doing some quick analysis, I found that the difference in just batting linear weights (haven't even gotten into running or fielding) between tranche 1 and tranche 2 in 2019 was about 6.5 runs, prorated across 650 PA. Between tranche 1 and tranche 3, it's 10.8 runs. The ability to shift those plate appearances up the ladder has some real value.

This part is important. We can also give credit to starters for the positions that they showed an ability to play, even if they didn't play them (this is the guy fully capable of playing center, but who's in a corner because the team already has a good center fielder) because he allows a team to carry a player who hits like a left fielder to functionally be the team's backup center fielder. He facilitates that movement upward among the tranches. We can start to appreciate the difference between a left fielder who would never be able to hack it in center (and the compensatory move that his team would have to make) and the left fielder who could do it, but just didn't have to very often.

Past that, you can continue to use whatever hitting and fielding and running metrics you like to determine a player's value, but when we get down to constructing that baseline, I'd argue we need a better conceptual and mathematical framework. It's going to require some more #GoryMath than we're used to, but I'd argue it's a better conceptualization of the way that MLB actually plays the game in 2020. If…y'know…MLB plays in 2020. If WAR is going to be our flagship statistic among the *acronymati*, then we need to acknowledge that it contains some old and starting-to-be-out-of-date assumptions about the game. We may need to tinker with it. Here's my idea for how.

—*Russell A. Carleton is an author of Baseball Prospectus.*

Secondhand Sport

by Patrick Dubuque

Back before time stopped, I liked to go to thrift stores. Now that I'm older, I rarely ever buy anything—I don't need much in my life, now—but I still enjoy the old familiar circuit: check to see if there are baseball cards to write about, look for board or card games to play with the kids, scan for random ironic jerseys, hit the book section. It takes ten, maybe fifteen minutes. Thrift stores are the antithesis of modern online shopping, because you don't know what they have, and you don't even really know what you want. It's junk, literal junk, stuff other people thought was worthless. That's what makes it great.

In an idealized economy, thrift stores shouldn't exist. Everybody has a living wage, and every product has a durability that exactly matches its desired life; nothing should need to be given away, no one should need to be given to. But then, thrift stores shouldn't work on a customer experience level, either. You wouldn't think an ethos of "let's make everything disorganized and hard to find" would lead to customer satisfaction, but low-budget retailers like TJ Maxx and Ross thrive on this model. People like bargain hunting as much for the hunting as the bargain; it's part of the experience, spending time as if it's a wager. There's a thrill, occasionally, in inefficiency.

In sports, the modern overuse of the word "inefficiency" is a condemnation: It insinuates that there is *an* efficiency, a correct way to be found, and that all other ways are wrong ways. It's prevalent in baseball but hardly contained to it; the lifehack, the Silicon Valley disruption are other examples of productivity creep in our daily lives. Their modern success makes plenty of sense. Maximization of resources, after all, is its own puzzle, and an industry of European board games is founded upon it. It's fun to take a system and optimize it, unravel it like a sudoku puzzle. If there's only one kind of genius, after all, there's no way anyone can fail to appreciate it.

Baseball has been hacking away at these perceived inefficiencies since its inception: platoons, bullpens, farm systems were all installed to extract more out of the tools at hand. But it's been a particular badge of the sabermetric movement, from Ken Phelps and his All-Star Team to Ricardo Rincon and the darlings of *Moneyball*. It's business, but it's also an ethos: the idea that there's treasure among the trash, something we all failed to appreciate until someone brought it to light.

It's the myth that made Sidd Finch so enticing, that fuels so many "best shape" narratives and new pitch promises. We all, athletes and unathletic sportswriters, want to believe that there's genius trapped inside us, and that it's just a matter of puzzling out the combination to unlock it. That our art, our style is the next inefficiency, waiting for our own Billy Beane. It's why we root for underdogs, and why we're excited for the Mike Tauchmans and the Eurubiel Durazos, champions of skin-deep mediocrity.

Except we aren't anymore, really. The days of "Free X" have descended beyond the ring of irony and into obscurity. There are still Xs to be freed, or at least one X, duplicated endlessly: Mike Ford, Luke Voit, Max Muncy. The undervalued one-dimensional slugger demonstrated how the game hasn't quite culturally caught up to its logical extreme. But for those who don't fit the rather spacious mold, times are grimmer. As Rob Arthur revealed several months ago, there's been a marked increase in the number of sub-replacement relievers. It's the outcome of a greater number of teams forced to play out games without the talent to win them, but it's also emblematic of the modern tendency of teams to dispose of their disposable assets, burning through cost-controlled arms the way that man chopped down forests in *The Lorax*. Stuff just isn't built to outlive their original owners anymore.

It's unsurprising, given how well-mined the market for inefficiencies has been of late. The disciples of the early analytics departments, and the disciples of those, have proliferated the league, with only a few backwater holdouts. The league has grown smarter, but every team has learned the same lesson. In fact, the phenomenon creates a peculiar kind of feedback loop: As teams value a specific subset of players or skills, prospective athletes learn to increase their own marketability by conforming themselves to the demands of their prospective employers.

And that's tragic, in the way that the extinction of animals is tragic; a certain amount of biodiversity in baseball has been lost. Shortstops hit like outfielders. Pitchers don't hit at all. Only the catchers remain idiosyncratic, thanks to the defensive demands of their position; eventually they too will be required to produce like everyone else, or they'll meet the fate of their battery mates. A perfect economy requires perfect production.

I mentioned earlier that more and more, I leave thrift stores empty-handed. It is true that I am more discerning than in the past; my bookshelves are full, and there are more streaming films than I will ever be able to watch. But there are other factors at play.

Thrift stores are, in a way, the bond markets of retail. When the economy is rough and other retailers are struggling, more people look secondhand for their products. But as recently as last year, publications were noting a reversal of the trend: Companies like Goodwill and Savers were expanding despite a strong economy. Publications credited a heightened sense of environmentalism and a rejection of cutting-edge fashion as drivers behind the increase, though the more likely answer is the modern American economy hasn't showered its favors equally, particularly among the young.

But it is more than just the economy. Baseball and thrift stores share something else in common, evident in our current conversations about re-starting the sport: They live in the gray area between public service and private enterprise. Thrift stores provide affordable necessities to lower-class citizens, and collectibles and fashion for the middle-class. Because of the success of the latter, prices have gone up across the board. Especially in terms of clothing, the middle-class flight from fashion into vintage has instead carried the aftereffects of fashion, including its costs, into a territory where people just want clothes. But there's another factor in the rise of prices, in the form of the internet.

The Goodwills of the world have grown smarter, too, employing the internet to extract full value from their detritus. Ebay, similarly, has lost much of the charm it had as a new frontier around the turn of the century. Everything has a price point now; even individual taste is no match for the algorithm, because anything rare, no matter how niche its market, is a collectible to someone.

The internet has had the same effect on thrift stores that sabermetrics has had on baseball; its equivalent to OBP was the bar scanner. As detailed in Slate, the rise of second-party stores on eBay and Amazon birthed an entire industry of used-good salespeople, armed with PDAs and scanners, buying books for three dollars to sell online for five. The author, Michael Savitz, reports earning $60,000 by working nearly 80 hours a week; he makes it clear that this is not a vocation of his choosing. It's long hours, with no real creativity or individuality, skimming the cream off of a local establishment and flipping it to someone with a little more money on the other side of the country. And once the vocation exists, the obvious question arises: why wait to put the wares out on the shelves? Why allow value to exist at all?

Nothing is ruined. Thrift stores will continue to sell polo shirts and DVDs, and baseball will continue to exist and make or lose money, depending on who you believe. But as we continue to refine our knowledge, we lose something in the conquest for efficiency, a delight born out of the unknown. The problem isn't the efficiency itself; we can't blame the booksellers, or the people sweeping freeways to collect grams of platinum from damaged catalytic converters. The problem is a system that requires this sort of profit-skimming behavior in order to feed families (or, for corporations, maximize shareholder return).

Houston Astros 2021

In times like these, with the 2020 season on the brink and the collective bargaining agreement close behind, it can often feel like the current situation is untenable. It can't keep going like this, even if we don't know what to do about it. But as with thrift stores, there's an equally irresistible feeling that it *has* to keep going, that it would be unimaginable to not have this broken, amazing sport. Both industries exist on an invisible foundation of friction, of chaos and unpredictability, even as both see their foundations buffed down to a perfect, untouchable polish. But if COVID-19 and its financial ramifications do, as some have suggested, make it such that the baseball that returns is fundamentally different than the baseball that came before, perhaps this is the time to lean in, and change the game even more. Fix bunting. Make defense more difficult. Create viable, alternate strategies. Add some chaos back into baseball. It's fun when no one knows quite where things are.

—Patrick Dubuque is an author of Baseball Prospectus.

Steve Dalkowski Dreaming

by Steven Goldman

We dream of being a pitcher, of starring in the major leagues. Depending on your age and your sense of historical perspective, you might imagine yourself as Walter Johnson, throwing harder than anyone else—hitting more batters than anyone else, too, but always feeling bad about it. You could picture yourself as a Tom Seaver or a David Cone, with all the stuff in the world but still being cerebral about it, thinking about so much more than burning 'em in there. There are so many models one could choose: You could be a Lefty Gomez, Jim Bouton, or Bill Lee, skilled, but not taking the whole thing too seriously, or a Lefty Grove, Bob Gibson, or Steve Carlton, powerful but treating each start like a mission to be survived instead of a game to be enjoyed.

Very few would dream of being Steve Dalkowski, the former Baltimore Orioles prospect who died of COVID-19 last week at the age of 80. Yet, there is something just as noble in Dalkowski's negative accomplishments—and accomplishments is what they are—as there is in the precision-engineered pitching of a Greg Maddux. You have to be very good to be that bad. Dalkowski had all of the stuff of the greatest pitchers but none of the command; his story is not one of failing to conquer his limitations, but striving against one of the cruelest hands that fate or genetics or personality can deal us: A desire to achieve great things which is almost but not quite matched by the ability to meet that goal.

As with Johnson, Grove, Bob Feller, and the rest of the hard-throwing pitchers who played before the advent of modern radar guns, we have to take the word of the players and coaches who saw Dalkowski pitch as to his velocity. He was a hard-drinking, maximum-effort pitcher who, if their memories are to be believed, consistently threw over 100 miles per hour. His was the Maltese Fastball, the stuff that dreams are made of. The problem is that velocity without command and control is still a good distance from utility. Dalkowski was the most effective towel you could design for a fish, the sleekest bathing suit intended to be worn by an astronaut, but that doesn't mean he wasn't beautiful: We can appreciate a journey even if it doesn't end at the intended destination.

Whether because of sloppy mechanics he couldn't calm, an inability to understand that a consistent 98 in the strike zone would likely be more effective than a consistent 110 out of it, or all that beer, Dalkowski could never make the adjustments that pitchers like Feller and Nolan Ryan made before him, possibly because he had so far to go: Feller, who never pitched in the minors, came up at 17 and spent three years walking almost seven batters per nine innings before settling in at 3.8 beginning when he was 20. Ryan started out walking over six batters per nine but gradually improved as his long career played out; for him to go from 6.2 walks per nine with the 1966 Greenville Mets to 3.7 with the 1989 Texas Rangers represents a 40 percent reduction. An equivalent improvement by Dalkowski would still have left him walking over 11 batters per nine innings.

Dalkowski was like *The Room* of pitchers, a player so bad he became good again. Cal Ripken, Sr., who both played with and managed Dalkowski, recalled in a 1979 *Sporting News* "where are they now" piece the occasion when the pitcher crossed up his catcher and his fastball, "hit the plate umpire smack in the mask. The mask broke all to pieces and the umpire wound up in the hospital for three days with a concussion. If they ever had a radar gun in those days, I'll bet Dalkowski would have been timed at 110 miles an hour."

Signed by the Orioles out of New Britain High in Connecticut in 1957, Dalkowski was sent to Kingsport in the Appalachian League, where he pitched 62 innings. He allowed only 22 hits in 62 innings, or 3.2 per nine, a number with no equivalent in major league history (though Aroldis Chapman came close in 2014), and also struck out 121 (17.6 per nine) and walked 129 (18.7). He was also charged with 39 wild pitches. That June, one of his fastballs clipped a Dodgers prospect named Bob Beavers and carried away part of his ear. "The first pitch was over the backstop, the second pitch was called a strike, I didn't think it was," Beavers said last year. "The third pitch hit me and knocked me out, so I don't remember much after that. I couldn't get in the sun for a while, and I never did play baseball again." Former minor leaguer Ron Shelton based the *Bull Durham* pitcher Nuke LaLoosh on Dalkowski. And yet, to see him as a figure of fun, an amusing loser, is to misunderstand something unique and strange.

Dalkowski kept on posting some of the strangest lines in baseball history. Pitching for the Stockton Ports of the Class C California League in 1960, he struck out 262 and walked 262 in 170 innings. Yet, he did improve, especially after pitching for Earl Weaver at Elmira in 1962. Weaver had previously had Dalkowski at Aberdeen in 1959, but wasn't ready to grapple with him then. This time he was. "I had grown more and more concerned about players with great physical abilities who could not learn to correct certain basic deficiencies no matter how much you instructed or drilled them," he related in his autobiography, *It's What You Learn After You Know It All That Counts*. He got permission from the Orioles to give all of his players the Stanford-Binet IQ test. "Dalkowski finished in the 1 percentile in his ability to understand facts. Steve, it was said to say, had the ability to do everything but learn." [sic]

IQ tests are problematic diagnostic tools, so take Weaver's estimate of Dalkowski's mental capabilities with a grain of salt. What's important is that even if he got to the right answer by way of the wrong reason, Weaver had learned something valuable. His insight was to stop asking Dalkowski to learn new pitches and just let him get by with the two that he had. Were Dalkowski a prospect today, that would have been a no-brainer: Can't develop a third pitch? The bullpen is right over there, sir. Player development wasn't like that then, but Weaver, temporarily Dalkowski's mentor, could let him work with what he had. According to Weaver, the pitcher responded: "In the final 57 innings he pitched that season Dalkowski gave up 1 earned run, struck out 110 batters, and walked only 11." It's not true—as per the *Elmira Star-Gazette*, as of late July, Dalkowski had walked 71 in 106 innings and finished with 114 in 160 innings, which means Dalkowski's control actually faded at the end of the season rather than improved—but that doesn't mean it didn't happen in some sense, just that it didn't happen that way. Again, it's the journey, not the destination, and his ERA was 3.04 so *something* had gone right.

Also along the way: The next spring, Orioles manager Billy Hitchcock was rooting for Dalkowski to make the team as a long-man—maybe Weaver had gotten through to him. There were things out of Weaver's control, like the universe's twisted sense of humor: that March, Dalkowski's elbow went "twang."

You sometimes read that it was the Orioles' insistence on Dalkowski learning the curve that did him in, but even if they hadn't learned their lesson, the injury was probably just a coincidence: Dalkowski had thrown an incredible number of pitches over the previous few years. Still, it testifies to the dangers of trying to get what you want and risking the loss of what you had. Dalkowski tried to come back, but the 110-mph stuff was gone. A pitcher with no control and no stuff is...a civilian. What followed were years of vagabond living, arrests for drunkenness. There were Alcoholics Anonymous meetings, assistance from baseball alumni associations, but none of it took. From the 1990s until the time of his passing he dwelt in an assisted living facility, suffering from alcohol-related dementia. He'd been a heavy drinker since his teenage years. As with all those pitches per game, there was a price to be paid. You make choices on the journey and some of them are irrevocable. It's like a fairy tale: "Bite of poison apple? Don't mind if I do."

In the aforementioned *Sporting News* profile, Chuck Stevens, the head of the Association of Professional Ballplayers of America, a ballplayer charity, said, "I've got nothing against drinking. I do it myself sometimes. But, I don't condone common drunkenness. We went through lots of heartache and many dollars, but Dalkowski didn't want to help himself and we weren't going to keep him drunk." The journey is *un*like a fairy tale: No one will come along and kiss it better, not if they're busy forming judgments.

In the end, we are left with a sort of philosophical chicken/egg conundrum: Is failing to meet your goals evidence of unfulfilled potential or the lack of it? Isn't what you did by definition what you were capable of doing? Or could you have broken through to something better with the right help, the right lucky break? These are unanswerable questions, and how we try to answer them may say more about us than about the people we're judging.

No pitcher ever has it easy. *All* pitchers must work hard. *All* pitchers must refine their craft. It's almost never just about *stuff*. Dalkowski dreaming is no insult to the great pitchers who made it; from Pete Alexander to Max Scherzer, they have all earned their way up. And yet, if it is true that we can only do as much as we can do, then the journey would be more of an adventure, the ultimate triumph or defeat more noble, if like Dalkowski we lacked 100 percent of the confidence, the command, the self-possession, the commitment, the resistance to making bad decisions that so many great players possess—to be gloriously human. Or, to put it more succinctly, it would be fun to be able to throw as hard as any person ever has. Even if just for a moment, and even if nothing more came of it than that, no one could say you hadn't lived life to the fullest.

—*Steven Goldman is an author of Baseball Prospectus.*

A Reward For A Functioning Society

by Cory Frontin and Craig Goldstein

On July 5, Nationals reliever Sean Doolittle said in the middle of a press conference regarding the restart of Major League Baseball and what would later be known as summer camp, "sports are like the reward of a functioning society." This sentence was amidst a much longer, thoughtful reply about the societal and health conditions under which MLB players were being brought back. It's a very similar sentiment to one Jane McManus used on April 7, when she discussed the White House's meeting with sports commissioners. She said "sports are the effect of a functioning society—not the precursor."

Both versions of the same sentiment spoke to a laudable ideal in the context of a country that was not addressing a rampaging virus, and opting instead to bring sports back for the feeling of normalcy rather than the reality of it. "Priorities," as McManus said.

On Wednesday, the NBA's Milwaukee Bucks conducted a wildcat/political strike, refusing to come out for Game 5 of their playoff series against the Orlando Magic. The Magic refused to accept the forfeit, and shortly thereafter other playoff series were threatened by player strikes. Eventually the league moved to postpone that day's games, folding to players leveraging their united power.

The backdrop against which these actions took place was the shooting by police of Jacob Blake. Blake was shot in the back seven times by police, as he attempted to get into his vehicle. He managed to survive the assault, but is paralyzed from the waist down.

⚾ ⚾ ⚾

The step taken to walk out, first by the Milwaukee Bucks, then subsequently by other NBA, WNBA, and MLB teams, was a step toward upholding the virtue of the sentiment described by McManus and Doolittle. But that sentiment does not align with the broad history of sports in this and other countries, a history that contradicts the core of the idealistic statement.

Sports have been a significant part of American society for most of its existence, expanding in importance and influence in recent years. The idea that society was functioning in a way that was worthy of the reward of sports for most of that time is laughable. Much of America is not functioning and has not functioned for Black people, full stop. The oppressed people at the center of this political act by players, specifically Black players, in concert throughout the NBA and in fits and starts throughout Major League Baseball, have not known a society that functions for them rather than *because* of them.

Politics has been part of the sports landscape since the inception of sport, but for just about as long people have bemoaned its presence. Sports are to be an escape, it is said. An escape from what, though? A functioning society?

No, the presence of sports has never signified a cultural or political system that is on the up and up. Rather, the presence of sports *reflect and reinforce the society* that produces them.

⚾   ⚾   ⚾

The Negro Leagues were born out of societal dysfunction. The need for entirely separate leagues, composed of Black and Latino players barred from the Major Leagues because of racism? That is not a functioning society, and yet there were sports.

Even the integration of players from the Negro Leagues resulted in a transfer of power and wealth from Black-owned businesses and communities and into white ones, mirroring the dysfunction that had bled into every aspect of American society at the time. Japheth Knopp noted in the Spring 2016 Baseball Research Journal:

> *The manner in which integration in baseball—and in American businesses generally—occurred was not the only model which was possible. It was likely not even the best approach available, but rather served the needs of those in already privileged positions who were able to control not only the manner in which desegregation occurred, but the public perception of it as well in order to exploit the situation for financial gain. Indeed, the very word integration may not be the most applicable in this context because what actually transpired was not so much the fair and equitable combination of two subcultures into one equal and more homogenous group, but rather the reluctant allowance—under certain preconditions—for African Americans to be assimilated into white society.*

To understand the value of a movement, though, is not to understand how it is co-opted by ownership, but to know the people it brings together and what they demand. When Jackie Robinson—the player who demarcated the inevitability of the end of the Negro leagues—attended the March on Washington for Jobs and Freedom in 1963, he did so with his family and marched alongside the people. He stood alongside hundreds of thousands to fight for their common civil and labor rights. "The moral arc of the universe is long," many freedom fighters have echoed, "but it bends towards justice." The bend, it is less frequently said, happens when a great mass of people place the moral arc of the universe on their knee and apply force, as Jackie, his family, and thousands of others did that day.

⚾   ⚾   ⚾

Of course, taking the moral arc of the universe down from the mantle and bending it is not without risk. Perhaps the outsized influence of athletes is itself a mark of a dysfunctional society, but, nonetheless, hundreds of athletes woke up on Wednesday morning with the power to bring in millions of dollars in revenues. That very power, as we would come to find out, was matched with the equal and opposite power to *not* bring those revenues. That power, in hands ranging from the Milwaukee Bucks, to Kenny Smith in the *Inside the NBA* Studio, from the unexpected ally, Josh Hader, and his largely white teammates to the notably Black Seattle Mariners, would be exercised for a single demand: the end to state violence against Black people. Not unlike the March itself, it sat at the intersection of the civil rights of Black Americans and bold labor action. The March on Washington stood in the face of a false notion of integration—against an integration of extraction but not one of equality—and proposed something different. Just the same, the acts of solidarity of August 26, 2020 will be remembered in stark defiance of MLB's BLM-branded, but ultimately empty displays on opening weekend.

Bold defiance like this can never be without risk. By choosing to exercise this power, the Milwaukee Bucks took a risk. They risked vitriol and backlash from those they disagreed with. They risked fines or seeing their contracts voided, as a walkout like this is prohibited by their CBA. They risked forfeiting a playoff game, one that, as the No. 1 seed in the playoffs, they'd worked all year to attain. They didn't know how Orlando would respond. It wasn't clear that other teams throughout the league would follow suit in solidarity. And it wasn't known the league would accept these actions and moderately co-opt them by "postponing" games that would have featured no players.

If the league reschedules the games, some of the athletes' risk—their shared sacrifice—will be diminished, in retrospect. But they did not know any of that when they took that risk. And it is often left to athletes to take these risks when others in society won't, especially those of their same socioeconomic status and levels of influence.

It is athletes, specifically BIPOC athletes, that take them, though, because they live with the risk of being something other than white in this country every day. They are no strangers to the realities of police brutality. It seems incongruous then, to say that sports are a reward for a functioning society when we rely on athletes to lead us closer to being a functioning society. Luckily, our beloved athletes, WNBA players first and foremost among them, understand what sports truly are: a pipebender for the moral arc of the universe.

—Craig Goldstein is editor in chief of Baseball Prospectus. Cory Frontin is an author of Baseball Prospectus.

Index of Names

Abreu, Bryan 80, 91
Altuve, Jose 16
Alvarez, Yordan 73
Báez, Pedro 39
Barber, Colin 92
Bielak, Brandon 41
Brantley, Michael 18
Bregman, Alex 20
Brown, Hunter 92
Castro, Jason 22
Cishek, Steve 43
Correa, Carlos 24
Dawson, Ronnie 74
Díaz, Aledmys 26
Dubin, Shawn 94
Garcia, Luis 45, 88
Greinke, Zack 47
Gurriel, Yuli 28
Hansen, Austin 94
Ivey, Tyler 94
James, Josh 49
Javier, Cristian 51
Jones, Taylor 75
Lee, Korey 90
Maldonado, Martín 30
McCormick, Chas 76, 95
McCullers Jr., Lance 53

Nova, Freudis 76, 91
Osuna, Roberto 81
Paredes, Enoli 55
Peacock, Brad 82
Pena, Jeremy 77, 88
Pressly, Ryan 57
Pruitt, Austin 82
Raley, Brooks 59
Reddick, Josh 33
Rodriguez, Nivaldo 61
Santos, Alex 83, 89
Scrubb, Andre 63
Smith, Joe 84
Sneed, Cy 65
Solis, Jairo 93
Solomon, Peter 94
Souza Jr., Steven 78
Stanek, Ryne 84
Straw, Myles 79
Stubbs, Garrett 80
Taylor, Blake 67
Toro, Abraham 35
Tucker, Kyle 37
Urquidy, Jose 69
Valdez, Framber 71
Verlander, Justin 85
Whitley, Forrest 86, 87

For the Joy of Keeping Score

THIRTY81 Project is an ongoing graphic design project focused on the ballparks of baseball. Since being established in 2013, scorecards have been a fundemantal part of the effort. Each two-page card is uniquely ballpark-centric — there are 30 variants — and designed with both beginning and veteran scorekeepers in mind. Evolving over the years with suggestions from fans, broadcasters, and official scorers, the sheets are freely available to everyone as printable letter-size PDFs at the project webshop: www.THIRTY81Project.com

Download, Print, Score, Repeat ...

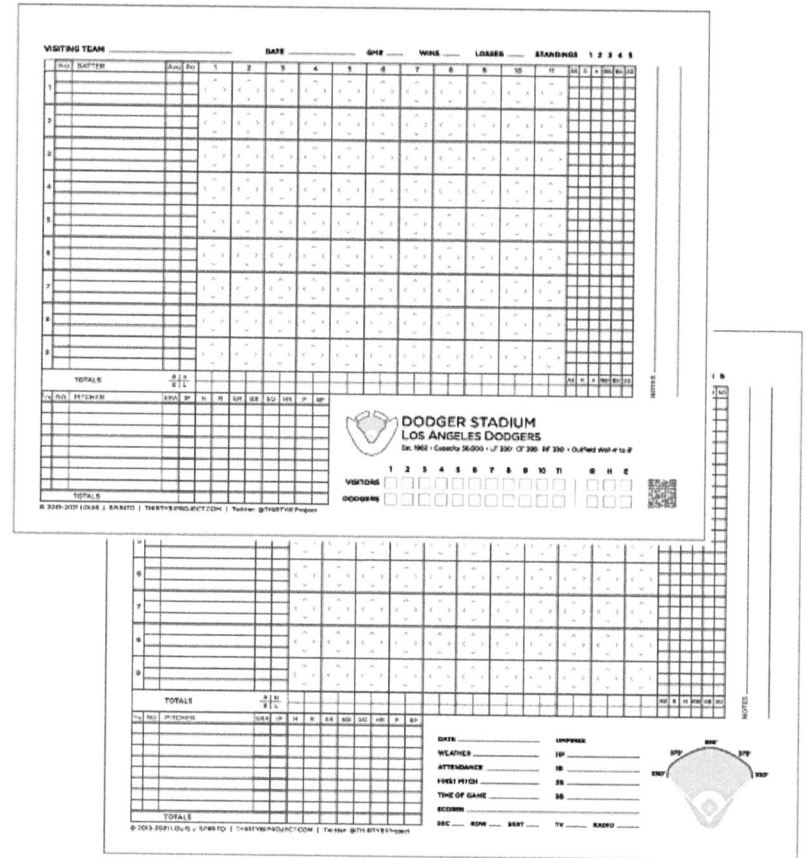

Scorecard design ©2013-2021 Louis J. Spirito | THIRTY81Project